P9-DFX-302

WALL
STREET
JOURNAL
BOOKS

NO CRUELER TYRANNIES

ACCUSATION, FALSE WITNESS, AND OTHER TERRORS OF OUR TIMES

DOROTHY RABINOWITZ

A WALL STREET JOURNAL BOOK

Published by Free Press

New York London Toronto Sydney Singapore

WALL STREET JOURNAL BOOKS

A WALL STREET JOURNAL BOOK
Published by Free Press
Rockefeller Center
1230 Avenue of the Americas
New York, NY 10020

FREE PRESS and colophon are trademarks
of Simon & Schuster, Inc.

The Wall Street Journal and the Wall Street Journal Book colophon
are trademarks of Dow Jones and Company, Inc.

For information about special discounts for bulk purchases, please contact
Simon & Schuster Special Sales:
1-800-456-6798 or business@simonandschuster.com

These articles were previously published individually in The Wall Street Journal.

DESIGNED BY LISA CHOVNICK

Manufactured in the United States of America

10 9 8 7 6 5 4 3 2 1

Library of Congress Cataloging-in-Publication Data

Rabinowitz, Dorothy.
    No crueler tyrannies : accusation, false witness, and other terrors of
our times / Dorothy Rabinowitz.
        p. cm.—(Wall Street journal book)
    "These articles were previously published individually in The Wall
Street journal"—T.p. verso.
    Includes index.
        1. Child sexual abuse—Investigation—United States.   2. Trials
(Child sexual abuse)—United States.   3. False testimony—United
States.   4. Child witnesses—United States.   5. Interviewing in child
abuse—United States.   6. Fells Acres Day Care (Firm)—Trials,
litigation, etc.   I. Title.   II. Series.

HV8079.C48swR33 2003
345.73'02536—dc21   2002044670

ISBN 0-7432-2834-0

CONTENTS

There is no crueler tyranny than that which is perpetrated under the shield of law and in the name of justice.

CHARLES-LOUIS DE SECONDAT,
BARON DE MONTESQUIEU, 1742

PREFACE

With two exceptions, the accounts that follow are of prosecutions that began in the 1980s, when the tide of mass child abuse cases had reached its height. In this period, the focus of suspicion fell mostly on child care workers, but the lightning of accusation would strike others as well as the fever of suspicion spread. That fever has since broken, but its effects have endured, thanks largely to the national publicity given to those early cases, with their terrifying details about children stabbed and assaulted by teacher-predators. The sexual abuse charge established itself as a force to be reckoned with, and not only in schools, as attorneys witnessing bitter custody battles today can attest. And though it is unlikely we will ever again see entire staffs of accused nursery school teachers paraded before TV cameras, prosecutions based on contrived testimony still take place regularly in quiet corners of the nation, and the prosecutors still win them, as they did recently in Troy, New York—a story included here.

These accounts are based for the most part on cases I first wrote about in The Wall Street Journal, beginning in 1995 with the first pieces on the Amirault family in Massachusetts. Everyone who writes for a newspaper knows what it is to want to say what has been left unsaid in a story—what there had been no space or time or opportunity to report.

This work provided the opportunity, particularly in the detailed sections on the Amiraults, to focus on the lives and character of some of these accused and to tell something also of their spouses, parents, and children cast into darkness along with them. It seems a long time since I began writing about these prosecutions, and it has been—a long time since the 1980s, when I first began looking into the strange charges brought against twenty-six-year-old Margaret Kelly Michaels, a teacher at a New Jersey nursery school. These cases invariably began with a single deadly accusation. Like lightning, the charge could strike anyone in an exposed position. Those most exposed to danger were child care workers, though the category of the vulnerable would in time expand to include people in all sorts of careers and situations.

The first case to raise alarms about predators in nursery schools was that involving the McMartin preschool in Manhattan Beach, California. It was not the first prosecution of its kind, but it was the one that would rivet the nation's attention. In August 1983, a woman named Judy Jones charged that twenty-five-year-old Ray Buckey, a teacher and grandson of the school's founder, had sodomized her two-year-old son. The parent who made the complaint was an alcoholic and was subsequently diagnosed as a paranoid schizophrenic. After her charge against Buckey (who was acquitted in 1990, along with his mother and school owner Peggy McMartin Buckey), she went on to make the same allegations about a member of the U.S. Marine Corps who had, she said, sexually assaulted her dog.

Details of astounding crimes supposedly committed at the school emerged from hundreds of interviews with McMartin pupils and became the stuff of daily headlines. Children were said to have been assaulted sexually with silverware, dragged off to cemeteries, terrorized into silence by being made to watch animals killed. A model of its kind, the case helped set the stage for other prosecutions, among them those of the Amiraults and Kelly Michaels and police officer Grant Snowden.

To no one do I feel more indebted than Bob Bartley, editor of the Journal, who recognized the moral significance of the Amirault case as soon as he read the first piece about the three members of a Massachusetts family, nursery school owners, imprisoned for nearly a decade. From that moment on, he offered unstinting encouragement, and space for that and all the similar investigations I undertook.

It would be hard to estimate all I owe to my colleague deputy editorial page editor Dan Henninger, who gave generously of his attention and imagination, who involved himself and followed, tirelessly, every development and legal turn in these cases. I am grateful to him and to my colleague Melanie Kirkpatrick, who asked questions, gave advice, and offered much the same help.

My thanks extend to colleagues in every quarter of The Wall Street Journal for the heartening support they gave over the years I spent writing about these cases.

Much has changed since the 1980s, when even the most sympathetic magazine editors quailed at the prospect of publishing a piece discrediting the charges against a convicted child molester. The exception was Harper's editor Lewis Lapham, who didn't require any persuading on the issue of false prosecutions and willingly took on my description, written before I joined the staff of The Wall Street Journal, of the Kelly Michaels case.

The first piece on the Amiraults, published January 1995, brought an enormous response from Wall Street Journal readers, who eventually would contribute tens of thousands of dollars to cover legal expenses for the effort to free the Amiraults. One Journal reader undertook payment of all fees to mount a new appeal for Miami police officer Grant Snowden, sentenced to five life terms. Another reader took it upon himself to pay the full four years of college tuition for Gerald Amirault's daughters, both of whom recently graduated.

For the attorneys who fought the appellate battles so brilliantly—attorneys like Robert Rosenthal, who lived mainly on Pop Tarts (the pay was minimal), Jamie Sultan, Daniel R.

Williams, and the late Morton Stavis—I can only record my boundless admiration.

I thank George Stavis, who wanted a way to carry on his father's work, and found it, and attorney Daniel Finneran.

To attorney Harvey A. Silverglate, my invaluable adviser on more matters than I can count, I owe my usual tremendous debt.

I thank Paul Gigot, Wall Street Journal editorial page editor, who encouraged me to take the time to write this book.

Seriously literate editors don't pack the offices of publishing houses these days. My thanks to Bill Rosen, my editor at Simon & Schuster, for being one—for his taste, inventiveness, and countless other contributions to this work.

I am grateful not least to Georges Borchardt, my literary agent, for his tough and discriminating eye, his enduring support and friendship.

NO
CRUELER
TYRANNIES

The Amiraults, Part One

In his early thirties, Gerald Amirault began to know what it meant to be content. He looked forward to the birth of a new child, the family business was thriving, and the promise of financial security lay ahead. The bustling Fells Acres Day School, which his mother had built in Malden, Massachusetts, grew more successful by the day. In all he could see a good life ahead for the family—for his wife, Patricia, their three children, and his younger sister, Cheryl, not to mention his sixty-year-old mother, Violet, who had made that future possible.

He had known Patricia—Patti to her family—since grade school, dated her throughout high school, and in 1977 they married, to nobody's surprise. Neither had spent much time looking at anyone else since their early teens; by that time,

Gerald was already, in a sense, wedded to Patti's entire family, particularly her parents, Mary and Phil McGonagle. They took him under their wing, invited him on vacations, directed him, protected him, and treated him, all in all, like a son.

Nothing brought Gerald greater happiness than the prospect of a fishing trip or some other outing with Phil and Mary and their four children. For the boy who carried in his heart the weight of a childhood haunted by terror of the beatings his drunken father regularly inflicted on Violet, Patti's boisterously happy household seemed a paradise. There, he absorbed a sense of life's possibilities. Above all, perhaps, he learned what a father could be.

Where mothers were concerned, he needed no models. Violet was as much mother as any ten sons could want, as Gerald came to know early in life. Like his younger sister, he basked in Violet's affection, a powerful force, particularly when it came to her beloved firstborn. As a child, he might elude his mother's efforts to discipline him, but never with any hope that he could succeed in fooling her. The less mischievous Cheryl was not so inclined to try, but had, like her brother, an early-developed sense of their mother as all-knowing, undeceivable, the one who could be depended on to make things come out right. She had taken them from the nightmare of their childhood and got them through to safety on years of welfare, food stamps, and her own labor. And— this was the thing that struck them when they were old enough to reflect on such things—she had made it all seem quite easy.

That sense of her powers lingered with Violet's children long into their adult lives—indeed, long after it became clear that there were some nightmares their mother could not end. Neither of them seemed to have absorbed Violet's assertiveness and flair for command, and in that they were content. Violet had enough for all of them. When they spoke of their mother in later years—when everything had gone to ruin—it was in tones of still-fresh wonder at all that she knew, all that she had done, and how she was able to manage in the midst of calamity.

There was a touch of the grandiose about Violet, no doubt about it. Everything there was to know about child rearing and development, she knew. Violet had read everything, knew all the latest theories, how things should and should not be done, and not only in her school. She worked endlessly, planned endlessly, and had infinite confidence in her perceptions of the world. In the darkest hours of her life as in the brightest, she could still project a remarkable air of authority.

People who knew Violet had no trouble understanding why Patti Amirault had trouble adjusting to a life influenced by her mother-in-law. Violet was not one to conceal her views on how the young couple should live and where. She even managed to dictate which house they should buy. Still, Gerald's wife came to terms with it all. She taught at Violet's school and went happily to her mother-in-law's weekly dinners, where family members and friends of the family stuffed themselves with a staggering variety of meat and pasta dishes. The same ferocious concentration Violet brought to her business went into her huge holiday parties and Sunday dinners. A master Italian cook, she did not lack for guests at her Sunday table.

Outside the family, people took note of her wardrobe, grown more opulent as her school began to prosper, and her cars, which were turned in for new models every year. In the eyes of some in Malden, Massachusetts, the fashionably turned-out Fells Acres principal and her daughter were lavish spenders. Those who thought that didn't know Violet, who relished style but only at the cheapest price. One of the world's dedicated shoppers, she knew quality and was prepared to spend any time necessary going through the racks to find it on sale. As for the year-old cars, she turned them in for new ones on the advice of her accountant, who taught her about depreciation.

She was, in fact, a frugal woman and far from a rich one. Many in Malden nonetheless thought of her as a woman of wealth, a view that didn't altogether displease Violet.

There was reason for frugality in a woman who had made her own way. Her husband, Francis Amirault, worked as a mechanic for General Electric when his drinking permitted.

He abandoned the family in due course, leaving Violet with two small children and no support. Under the circumstances, neither his wife nor his children mourned his departure. His attacks on Violet had become more frequent and violent, his alcohol binges longer and more threatening. As Violet discovered, it was no use calling the authorities for help. The police responded to her calls by sending her husband's brother, a member of the force, whose mission it apparently was to quiet Francis down and keep it in the family. No arrest was ever made, however bruised and bloody Violet appeared when the police car rolled up, and she expected none.

On Christmas morning in 1963, the children crept downstairs early, looking for their presents. They found instead a terrifying bedlam: Violet trying to shield herself from her husband's fists. As he had done before, the not-quite-eight-year-old Gerald began pummeling his father and jumping on his back to try to stop the beating. It was the last such Christmas morning the Amiraults would spend this way. Shortly after this episode, Violet's husband left the house for good. His children never saw him again, but they heard that he had entered a hospital suffering delirium tremens. They learned of his death in 1983 in the same way.

Intent on staying home with Cheryl and Gerald, Violet baby-sat for the neighbors' children to supplement her welfare checks. At night, she went off to MIT to study and earn a certification in child care. On certain days, after Violet had picked Cheryl up from grade school, as she always did, the two would go to stand in line for the cheese and other food supplements given to the needy. A prolific inventor of games and all manner of diversions, Violet could make such occasions fun for a child. There may have been no money for toys, but Cheryl and Gerald did not lack for entertainment. Their mother saw to that. A neighborhood house was being moved, she might announce, as she rushed the children over to the site. They were going off to an adventure, she instructed them. And an adventure they would have, as Violet pointed out every detail of the great drama unfolding before them.

In 1983, Cheryl, a Fells Acres teacher, married Al, Gerald's friend. A joyful Violet saw her daughter walk up the aisle of the Immaculate Conception Church. Everywhere around her sat Fells Acres pupils ecstatic at the sight of the bride. The whole school had been invited to the service, and the whole school seemed to have turned out.

Her children safely settled, her school a success, Violet could not have asked for more than she now had. She could not have dreamed, either, how quickly it could be taken.

On Labor Day 1984, roughly a year later, Violet received a call about a child abuse accusation made against her son, who helped manage Fells Acres. Two days later, the police arrested Gerald on charges that he had raped a five-year-old boy, a new pupil.

———

The case began when the parent filed a complaint against thirty-one-year-old Gerald. The charge had its origins in an incident that had taken place months earlier. In April, an aide had informed Gerald that the child needed attention; he had wet his pants. Gerald changed the boy's underpants and delivered the soiled garment to his house.

Shortly after, the child's mother began brooding about certain behavioral problems, bed-wetting among them. In the rash of media stories about child molestation, bed-wetting ranked high among the symptoms parents were told to watch for. Preoccupied by this worry, she instructed the boy he should have no fear of talking about anything like that and told him that her own brother had been abused. The uncle then questioned the boy, who reported that Gerald had taken his pants down.

For the next four months, the child's mother questioned him, fruitlessly. She then took him to see a psychologist, who recorded no mention of Gerald in the boy's responses. By September, however, the child had begun to talk about a secret room and sexual acts Gerald had him perform each day he was at the school—nineteen days in all—and to say that he had been forced to drink urine.

The mother made her call to the abuse hot line. Two days later, the police came to the school to collect the class lists. They gave no answer to the stream of furious questions Violet put to them. The next day, the police arrested Gerald. Within hours, Phil McGonagle was at the station house, bent on a face-to-face talk with his son-in-law. If there was the slightest chance any of this could be true, he wanted to know, he told Gerald. The broad-shouldered firefighter looked into his son-in-law's eyes and heard what he had to say. He knew, almost at once, that he would never again have to consider such a question. There would be no more passionate enlistees in the battle to free Gerald Amirault than his mother- and father-in-law. They were in for a long term of service.

Less than a week after Gerald's arrest, the State Office for Children closed Violet's school. She was at this point well into her search for lawyers to represent Gerald and the school. She was soon to discover, after finding them, that there was no money to pay them. Less than a month after the first reports about alleged child sex abuse at the school, a Fells Acres parent put a lien on all of Violet's property and on Gerald's house. To get it lifted, Violet had to agree to an outright payment to the parent of $50,000. The same parent would later receive an insurance settlement of nearly $2 million.

Even so, the Amiraults were certain that all would come right and soon. In this, they were like most others in their situation. Dazed though they might be at the accusations, the invasion by investigators, and the initial arrests, in their minds they were clear about one thing: at any moment, the authorities would rush forward to announce they had made a mistake.

The Amiraults found, immediately after the first accusation, that talk or explanations from them were apparently the last thing anyone connected with the investigation wanted. In short order, the hideous sex crimes Gerald had supposedly committed began to multiply, as did the number of the accused. According to new allegations, Violet herself, now sixty years old, and Cheryl, age twenty-six, had committed monstrous sexual crimes against children ages three to five. To the family's consternation, the police asked them no questions.

For days, Cheryl and Violet went to the Malden police station looking for someone to talk to them. The answer they invariably received was that the police had nothing to tell them and that they would be informed of anything they needed to know.

In fact, the police were now busy instructing Fells Acres parents. Ten days after the hot-line call accusing Gerald, the police called the parents to a meeting. Eighty showed up at the station house auditorium, where the police informed them that there were certain symptoms of child abuse they should look for, among them bed-wetting, nightmares, fighting, and loss of appetite. They were told to go home and ask their children particularly about a magic room, a secret room, and a clown. They were instructed that they should not accept at face value a child's denial that he or she had been molested. Above all, warned Detective John Rivers, "God forbid you say anything good about the people [the Amiraults] or your children will never tell you anything."

The parents went home and duly began to ask about the magic room, the secret room, and a clown. In between, the parents called one another and exchanged word of their progress.

———

State prosecutors building these high-profile cases well understood the problems posed by the strange charges and the fantasy-riddled narratives of the child plaintiffs. How could they make credible to jurors the extraordinary prowess of defendants who could assault whole classes of preschoolers daily, dressing and undressing twenty or more, all accomplished in a half hour's time, in a busy school, with no one noticing, no child ever sent home with mismatched socks?

This was a problem whose solution required the attention of specialists. Jurors had to be given a reason to believe that four year olds could be raped with butcher knives that left them uninjured, could be tied naked to trees and raped in broad daylight in front of a school facing the street and before the entire school population, as Violet Amirault would be accused and convicted of having done.

The state's solution lay with their experts—witnesses who could explain and render such mysteries comprehensible.

In the 1987 trial of Margaret Kelly Michaels, the New Jersey prosecutors had employed Eileen Treacy, a much-traveled New York abuse expert who had at her command a list of some thirty-two behavioral indicators of child abuse. She had as well a theory explaining what children really meant when they said they had not been touched. She would become the prosecutor's most important witness.

Prosecutors and trials were far from Kelly Michaels's mind when the detectives came knocking on her door on a May morning in 1985. The twenty-four-year-old former teacher at the Wee Care Day Nursery in Maplewood, New Jersey, who viewed police as benevolent protectors, put the whole matter down to some confusion. She willingly accompanied the detectives to the station house and answered all questions, certain someone would soon make a phone call or a revelation that would clear everything up. She agreed to waive her *Miranda* rights, passed a lie detector test, and spent the day answering questions. By now shaken, she went home to her parents in Pittsburgh, where she placed intermittent, inquiring, and mostly unproductive phone calls to the Maplewood police to check on her status. Within a few months, the investigators concluded that Kelly Michaels had, in her seven months at the school, molested and terrorized all fifty-one of the pupils. In December 1985, a grand jury handed down an indictment charging 235 counts of abuse against thirty-one children.

The case against her had its beginnings in a doctor's visit. A four-year-old Wee Care pupil having his temperature taken rectally at his pediatrician's office announced that his teacher, Kelly, also took his temperature. The nurse and the child's mother began to ask questions. Ten days later, the detectives arrived at Kelly Michaels's door.

The story of the young teacher ultimately charged with 131 counts of sex abuse against twenty children, ages three to five, soon had the New Jersey press agog. It looked to be the most sensational case ever to fall to prosecutor Glenn Goldberg. Jut-jawed and confident, Goldberg had a taste for trial theatrics, which he carried off with some flair.

To show that Kelly Michaels lied about all sorts of things, including taking music lessons, Goldberg demanded at trial that the defendant play the piano in the courtroom. The prosecutor himself erupted in song at one point while holding forth on the lyrics of a Bob Dylan song discovered in one of the teacher's notebooks. The lyrics, which she had copied into her notebook, included references to a lover who had walked out the door and "taken all his blankets from the floor"—a significant clue, Goldberg said, to Kelly Michaels's criminal sexual inclinations. The nursery school children, he told jurors, also slept on blankets and mats.

The prosecutor's office left nothing to chance. Months before the indictment against Kelly Michaels came down, assistant prosecutors instructed parents in the preparation of charts and diaries listing the symptoms of abuse they had noticed in their children. Huge stacks of these charts filled the prosecutors' offices.

When a five-year-old witness claimed during the trial that she had been "tractored" by Kelly—that is, put inside a tractor with other children and assaulted there—the prosecutors went to work. Eager to substantiate this claim, they brought a representative of the Maplewood street maintenance department to give testimony that a tractor had been parked in the vicinity of the school.

They would have confronted a greater challenge substantiating much of the other testimony the children gave. One five-year-old boy informed the court that Kelly had turned him into a mouse while he was in an airplane on the way to visit his grandmother.

After nearly two and a half years of rehearsal and other

work with the prosecutors, some of the young witnesses still changed stories on the stand or denied they had been abused. One told the court that Kelly made him push a sword in her rectum.

The attorneys and the judge then entered into a lengthy and earnest colloquy on whether the instrument was a sword or a saw. Once this was resolved, the child continued, telling the court that after he had done as Kelly had directed, she told him to take it out.

"What did Kelly say when you took the sword out?" came the question.

"She said, 'Thank you.'"

The tapes of the childrens' initial interrogations showed that most had no idea what the interviewer was talking about; most had nothing to say or simply denied that anything had happened to them.

Prosecution expert Eileen Treacy explained. A child's emphatic denial that anything had happened was *in fact* proof that the child had been victimized, she informed the jury. Citing the theory of the child abuse accommodation syndrome, she described its various phases. If children gave a succession of "no" answers when asked if they had been abused, that was, Treacy explained, "proof of the suppression stage."

This expert witness also interpreted the data in the parents' charts and diaries. Lacking physical and any other material evidence, the prosecutors instead exhibited the piles of parents' charts listing the abuse symptoms they had noticed in their children. A cornerstone of the state's evidence, the charts listed bed-wetting, nightmares, and changes in behavior—all symptoms the parents had been told to watch for in their initial meetings with the state's experts.

Other signs raised ominous suspicions, among them the lack of appetite for peanut butter. Accusations against the defendant included the charge that she spread peanut butter on the children's bodies, particularly the genitals, which she then licked off. "Child won't eat peanut butter" was one of the most frequently cited items in symptom charts the parents compiled—proof, the prosecutors pointed out, of the trauma Kelly Michaels had inflicted on the children.

Another lack-of-appetite item led to the same conclusion, said Treacy. A parent noted that her child no longer cared for tunafish. This had significance, Treacy told the jurors: "It's well known that the smell of tuna fish is similar to the odor of vaginal secretions."

But for variations in detail, the defendant stood accused of sexual crimes much like those charged in other such cases around the country. Here too was a secret room; here too children were given magic "truth drinks"; and here too children questioned by investigators named every teacher at the school as being present at the torture sessions.

In the tranquil setting of the day school, which occupied several floors of Maplewood's largest Episcopal church, Kelly Michaels had allegedly raped the children with knives, forks, and Lego blocks and a large wooden cooking spoon. She had made the children drink her urine and eat cakes of feces and forced them, under threat of death, to play games in the nude.

For those harboring doubts that this one woman could commit so many crimes, so terrible in their brutality, assistant prosecutor Sara McArdle provided a historical parallel. In her summation, she reminded the jury that Adolf Hitler, "one man," had persecuted not one little school but the entire world—"Jews, Gypsies, Czechs, and blacks." It required no expert to explain the prosecutor's strange inclusion of blacks on her list of Hitler's prime victims; many of the jurors were black.

Despite the daily horrors their teacher had allegedly inflicted, the Wee Care children showed sorrow when she left the school after seven months to work elsewhere, and they eagerly asked when they could see her again. This, Treacy explained, was all part of the abuse syndrome: if children felt they had a relationship with the teacher, "that fits into the engagement phase."

The jurors took thirteen days to come in with a guilty verdict on 115 counts of abuse. The defendant was declared not guilty of the one charge that started the whole thing—the rectal thermometer accusation. It had not occurred to the four year old to mention that the temperature taking his teacher had done was with a plastic strip on the forehead. That first charge was nonetheless fatal, bringing on, as invariably happened in these cases, a rapidly multiplying number of others—more and more accusations, more victims.

Kelly Michaels was sentenced a few months later to forty-seven years in prison.

Her prospects for a successful appeal seemed, at best, grim when she was dispatched to a protective custody cell in the high-security women's prison in Clinton, New Jersey. The Michaels family had no money for private appellate attorneys. The state provided an appellate attorney who offered advice she angrily refused. She could plead guilty, which would give her a chance to get out, maybe in time to have a couple of kids of her own.

Two years passed before she had any serious prospect of rescue. That came, finally, when civil rights attorney Morton M. Stavis decided to take the case pro bono. In the course of this endeavor, Stavis received his first education in the attitudes such causes engendered in his own political world. He would discover that the New York–based Center for Constitutional Rights, which he had helped to found—an agency emphatically devoted to left-of-center causes—wanted nothing to do with this case. Arguing for due process on behalf of a person charged with child sex abuse violated the politically progressive views held by many at the center. This case was, they told Stavis, all wrong for them.

Such attitudes toward child abuse cases—toward, indeed, all crimes involving special categories of victims like women and children—were not uncommon. In the late 1980s, as today, there was a school of advanced political opinion of the view that to take up for those falsely accused of sex abuse charges was to undermine the battle against child abuse; it was to betray children and all other victims of sexual predators. To succeed in reversing the convictions in such cases was to send a discouraging message to the victims and to encourage predators.

Where advanced reasoning of this sort prevailed, the facts of a case were simply irrelevant. What mattered was the message—that such crimes were uniquely abhorrent and must be punished accordingly.

This was not a view that a seasoned constitutional lawyer like Morton Stavis could understand: innocence was innocence, violations of due process just what the words meant and precisely what the center's work was supposed to be about. Still, founder or no founder, he was not a man to throw his weight around. Eschewing arguments with the center staff, he said nothing, packed up the case files, assembled a group of law students, and spent the next years working on the Michaels case from his Manhattan apartment.

In time, the Center for Constitutional Rights would change its view and donate much effort distributing defense funds for the accused in similar cases. That change had something to do, no doubt, with the outcome of the Michaels case. Stavis did not live to see his victory. Aided by young lawyers Daniel R. Williams, principal writer of the brief, and Robert Rosenthal, he had spent close to four years on the appeal. Within weeks of the completion of the appellate brief, the seventy-seven-year-old attorney died suddenly.

It was now necessary to find a replacement to make the oral argument before the justices of the New Jersey Appeals Court. This problem was solved, in a fashion, when William Kunstler stepped in—Stavis's old friend, if also a figure whose political attitudes Stavis had more and more come to detest. Kunstler offered to join the then very new law school graduate Robert Rosenthal in the argument before the court, and an odd couple they made—the tall, flamboyantly confident Kunstler, who knew virtually nothing about the case, and young Rosenthal, making his first appearance before a court.

None of it would matter. The justices knew the case, had read the briefs, and knew what they thought. It was not long before everyone in the hearing room knew what they thought as well. Kelly Michaels's mother, Marilyn, and Stavis's widow, Esther, sat clutching hands, eyes widening in disbelief, as the justices began evidencing their barely concealed scorn for the prosecutor's case—and their expert witness, in particular.

This was a wholly new experience for the Michaels defense, as for Kelly Michaels's family. Neither had ever before seen the state prosecutors or their evidence treated with anything but reverence. Judge William Harth, who had presided over Michaels's trial, had made no secret of his sympathies. He had dandled the young witnesses on his lap. He denied the defense psychologist the right to cross-examine the children, as the prosecution's psychologist had been able to do, on the grounds that being asked questions a second time could traumatize the young witnesses. Unstinting in his concern for the plaintiffs' privacy, the judge strictly limited defense investigation into the family background of the accusers, and to protect the anonymity of the children, he sealed the trial transcript.

But at the oral argument, the prosecutors found themselves having to answer questions like, "Do you actually consider this evidence?"

It was well known, the prosecutor told the justices, in an argument familiar to anyone who had attended any such trial, that children did not lie about sex abuse.

"Are you trying to bamboozle this court?" a justice asked

her. He and his fellow justices had accumulated many years of experience on the bench. They were not easily bamboozled, the justice informed her.

When the session ended, journalists and television crews came racing to congratulate the Michaels family and the attorneys. Never had they witnessed an oral argument that left so little doubt as to what the justices' final decision would be. That decision came a few months later when the court indeed vacated the conviction and set Kelly Michaels free. She had spent, in all, five years in prison.

Margaret Kelly Michaels married Jay Romano, a New Jersey judge and a writer for The New York Times, not long after her release. She had come out in time to have her couple of kids, the appellate attorney's warnings notwithstanding. In 2001, she gave birth to Max, her fourth child. A fifth is on the way.

———

Gerald Amirault spent one night in prison before being released on bail, just in time to attend the birth of his son. Sitting with his wife at the hospital, he looked up to see his face on the small television screen. A reporter was delivering an update on the latest news, gathered from the prosecutor's office, on the crimes charged to the Amiraults. The Fells Acres story had begun its long run on the local news. Soon—and it was a fact that had the power to shock him for a long time to come—he had reason to fear walking into a store and being recognized. More than one woman had screamed in terror at the sight of him. He was shocked because of all three Amiraults, he was the one most persistent in the belief that the huge error would soon unravel, and they would go on about their lives again. But Violet had followed all the stories about child care workers put on trial around the nation, and she was far more fearful, in ways she tried not to share with the children.

The newly married Cheryl—now Cheryl Amirault LeFave—tried to lose herself in work. When the state authorities closed Fells Acres, she found a clerical job in which she could immerse herself. Unable to bear the humiliation of the nightly news coverage about the Amiraults, the daily blast of headlines and details of the sex crimes charged to the family, to her—she had taken a job as far from Malden as possible.

Even so, strangers would often recognize her on the street. She found that she could maintain her composure—except for one sort of encounter. All control vanished when, as happened often enough, someone walked up to her on the street and offered a kind word. It was the kindness that undid her, she soon learned—the comforting hand that triggered an onslaught of tears.

It was clear, after the first accusation that Labor Day weekend, that nothing in the Amiraults' heretofore abundant and busy existence would ever be the same again. Violet's school was closed permanently long before any of the Amiraults were put on trial. According to the official ruling, the school was to be closed because pupils had been molested in a magic room.

With the school closed, Gerald had to find a way to earn money. With prosecutors preparing a case against him, the trial a long way off, he looked for work, but always in vain. The Amirault name and his face were by now too well known. Finally, a friend who managed a local sports arena cast caution aside and hired Gerald. The job lasted no more than a night; outraged patrons made their feelings known as soon as they recognized the face they had so often seen on their TV screen. With apologies, the manager threw his hands up. Gerald left willingly, crushed by the screams of horror he evoked. After that he didn't like to leave the house except when absolutely necessary.

He was not without sources of solace. He had Patti and the children, on whom he doted, and Phil and Mary. There was less comfort to be found among the other accused in the family. Gerald, his sister, and his mother clung to one another, but their old closeness was now a haunted thing. As their humiliation grew with the daily more terrible stories about their sexual torture of children, their ease with one another grew less. Some days Cheryl could not bear to look into her mother's eyes. She could not look into those of her brother. Each knew the torment of the other, and it was too much to behold.

———

The accusations against the Amiraults came at the height of a wave of high-profile child abuse cases that swept the country in the 1980s, one of the earliest of which was the now-notorious McMartin preschool case in California. The nation would not fail to be mesmerized by the televised images of the frightened middle-aged to elderly nursery school teachers, mainly women, led out in cuffs and accused of sexual crimes hitherto undreamed of. It was not for nothing that prosecutors in other such cases stressed that their case was nothing like the McMartin prosecution. In fact, the children's testimony in the Amirault case and the charges built on them were, give or take a few details, virtually identical to those in McMartin and others around the nation. Given all the abuse investigators pressing children for information about secret rooms and clowns and the like, it could hardly have been otherwise.

True, there was a certain epic grandeur about the Mc-

Martin case, which involved claims of abuse in underground tunnels, molestation in hot-air balloons, and similar marvels. Even as late as the mid-1990s, die-hard believers among the plaintiff parents were still to be found at the school site, faithfully conducting their searches for the underground tunnels.

That the wave of spectacular child abuse trials emerged in the 1980s was no accident. It had certainly been helped along by the Mondale Act of 1979—legislation that brought a huge increase in funds for child protection agencies and legions to be employed as abuse investigators. The increase in agencies and staffs soon begat investigations and accusations of child abuse on a grand scale.

Once an investigation began and a case was in the making, the state seldom had trouble finding parents ready to believe the charges. The targets of prosecution in these cases could usually find support among family members and close friends, but rarely among the clients of the nursery school, and for good reason. The pressure to join forces to win conviction was great, the rewards of dissent slender. If there were parents who harbored doubts about the truth of the charges, they generally kept it to themselves. There were also exceptions. From the time the Amiraults were first accused, one small knot of parents remained steadfastly unconvinced that the proprietors of Fells Acres had terrorized and tortured their children. Still, the Fells Acres case yielded a few vocal doubters. Parent Deborah Hersey told a reporter that her schedule made it necessary to keep popping up at the school unexpectedly. She or her husband was forever showing up at odd times. "There were no locked doors, no secret rooms, the atmosphere was wide open, nobody escorted us." Violet would tell them to go find the boy, usually with apologies for being too busy to accompany them.

Hersey's doubts increased after the meetings police held with the parents. As far as she was concerned, police inspector John Rivers's main purpose was to convince her that her child had been molested. After the interview, she wondered uneasily what would have happened if she had been a touch more gullible. Or less afraid to tell him what she thought.

Exceptions notwithstanding, the prosecutors found no lack of parents ready to sign on as plaintiffs against Fells Acres. First one and then another parent joined the list of those alleging that the Amiraults had raped and terrorized their children. What happened to their children at Fells Acres was now the sole preoccupation of the families, the sole topic of discussion. Each day brought details of new crimes charged to the Amiraults, now the subject of daily headlines. Children had been raped with knives and sharp sticks and had been assaulted by a clown (alleged to be Gerald) in a "magic room." After long sessions with investigators, children told of being forced to drink urine, of watching the Amiraults slaughter bluebirds, of meeting robots with flashing lights. Violet stood accused of shoving a stick into the rectum of a child standing in front of her and had raped him with a magic wand. Later, the same child testified that he was tied naked to a tree in the schoolyard, in front of all the teachers and children, while "Miss Cheryl" cut the leg off a squirrel. Gerald's nickname, Tooky (given by Violet in honor of a favorite piece of his infant babble), took on ominous overtones. A name that evoked no one human, that could be made to sound spooky, and that seemed suitable for a malignant pied piper in clown costume who lured children into danger.

Early in the development of the first case—Gerald's—the prosecutors told reporters that they were seeking evidence of child pornography. Local papers soon carried news of twenty-nine photographs and of a camera seized at the school. As it turned out, the pictures were unremarkable—the routine stuff of school celebrations, birthday parties, and the like. The prosecutors next undertook a global search for pornographic material linked to the Amiraults, also fruitless.

The issue was of some importance to the prosecutors, confronted with the necesssity of finding a motive for the wholesale assaults on children, all of which were alleged to have taken place during the last two years of the school's operation. The Fells Acres Day School had been in existence for twenty years, in which time it had acquired a sterling reputation. The waiting list of those trying to get a place at the school was long.

In those twenty years, there had been no record of complaint. When the charges against the Amiraults became major news, no word came from anyone claiming to have been victimized earlier. Of the thousands of children who had graduated from Fells Acres prior to the last two years, none had any stories of abuse to tell.

The prosecutors had to contend, moreover, with the problem posed by their picture of Violet Amirault. Thus far, it was that of a successful woman who had at the age of sixty taken to raping small children and terrorizing them into silence. There had to be a more reasonable picture. One solution would be the child pornography motive, with the Amiraults portrayed as profiteers and manufacturers—a suggestion the prosecutors began developing in the first weeks of the investigation.

It was during this period that the school's teachers were grilled at length, but none could say they saw anything wrong going on at the school. One or two disliked Violet. Still, they could come up with no suspicion or clue, frightened though they were by the police, who told them they were lying and suggested that they too could be implicated in the crimes that had taken place at the school. One of

the aides later recalled her own fervent effort to think of
something to tell the police that might satisfy them—some
abnormality. She could not for the life of her think of anything.

But while police interrogated the teachers and searched
for child pornography, the main work of the prosecution was
taking place in the offices where the Fells Acres children were
interrogated. As interview records confirm, no worker was
more tireless than pediatric nurse Susan Kelley.

Confronted by children who said nothing had happened, she was prepared to persist. Persistence was everything in the development of charges. The rule of thumb
guiding child interviewers in these cases was a simple one: if
children said they had been molested, they were telling the
truth; those who denied they had been abused were not
telling the truth and were described as "not ready to dis-
close," a phrase that appeared quite often in the interviews of
the Fells Acres children.

Although they had been questioned at home for weeks
about a magic room and a clown, the children had little or
nothing to say about these things. Asked if something bad
had happened they wanted to tell, children said repeatedly
that nothing had happened. Here was a dilemma for the interviewer. Confronted with obstructions to the goal at hand,
to get a disclosure, Nurse Kelley promised rewards if the
children talked about the bad things. She assured them that

some of their friends had already told about the bad things and that they could help too if they would tell. The helping theme was central to these interrogations. It called on the child to tell, because telling would mean helping other children, the interviewers, and the child's parents, and it would give the child a chance to catch up with other children, who, Susan Kelley informed them, had already helped everyone out by telling.

Even with these enticements, it would take time and all Nurse Kelley's persistence to get a child to say something that bore any resemblance to a disclosure. In the early interviews—before the children had undergone numerous interrogations calling on them to help by talking about something bad the clown did, or Miss Vi or Cheryl did—children clung to what they knew. Some recalcitrants continued to defend their own memory of events for a long time and thwarted the interviewer.

Nurse Kelley told one Fells Acres child that her friend Sara had said, "The clown had you girls take your clothes off in the magic room."

CHILD: No, she's lying.

NURSE: She's lying? Why would she lie about something like that?

CHILD: We didn't do that.

Next, the interviewer told the child, "I really believed her [Sara] because she told me all about it, and she even told me what the clown said."

CHILD: What was it?

Another child showed anger at the repeated questions and at the fact, obvious enough to a five year old, that her answers were not being accepted. In the course of the interview, the girl said more than a dozen times that Gerald had not touched her sexually.

INTERVIEWER: Did anybody touch Penny [the child's friend] on her bum?

CHILD: Nobody. Nobody didn't do it.

Four more times the interviewer asked if anybody had touched the children. Four more times the child said no.

Asked yet again, the child finally erupted, "Nobody didn't do it!"

Nurse Kelley did not fail to let these children know one way or another that their responses grieved her. Still, her air of disappointment was mingled with forgiveness and the suggestion that all could still be well if the child decided to tell. The door was always open. After an interview in which a child named Jennifer repeatedly denied that she had been molested, Nurse Kelley held a meeting with the girl's parents. She informed them that in her view, Jennifer had been sexually abused and required therapy.

Parents receiving such news from a person designated as an authority on the subject would not be inclined to dismiss it, and these did not. They became, indeed, the most active of plaintiffs against the Amiraults, certain that their daughter had suffered atrocious assaults at Fells Acres and certain that all the ills to befall her and the rest of the family for the next twenty years of their lives stemmed from this crime.

Nurse Kelley assured their stubborn child that the door was open. "I just want you to know that if you ever decide that you do want to come and talk to me about AJ [the child's friend] and the clown, that you could tell your mommy and your mommy would bring me back to talk to you, okay?"

To get at the problem of children who had nothing to say about abuse—and this was true of all of them, even after hours of multiple interrogations by the police and Department of Social Service workers—Nurse Kelley employed Bert and Ernie puppets and dolls. The dolls came with conspicuously detailed sexual organs, the better to focus the child's mind on the issue of importance. Still, when the interviewer asked a child to show where on the doll the clown had touched her, uncomprehending children offered the wrong sorts of answers. "On the foot," for example, was of no help.

With repeated questioning, the novelty of the dolls soon waned for the Fells Acres children. One bored child wanted no more of the doll. Nurse Kelley told the girl she could not put the doll away until she showed where else the clown touched her. By way of response, the child threw the doll, exclaiming, "He did this"—a tactic that effectively persuaded the interviewer to end this inquiry for the moment.

There were, in any case, numerous other techniques that might be employed in order to get children to make disclosures. Some took a good deal of time. Having heard that a child—otherwise not forthcoming about details of abuse—had mentioned an elephant game to her parents, Nurse Kelley took up the theme, a promising one to the abuse investigator. Talk of games conjured visions of disclosures, perhaps multiple disclosures, about Gerald or Violet Amirault in costume, committing sexual outrages—getting a child to lick ice cream off the elephant's tail perhaps. In the games envisioned by the investigators, this would translate into Gerald's penis.

"Was this a real elephant or somebody dressed up as an elephant?" Nurse Kelley asked the child.

CHILD: Somebody dressed up.

KELLEY: Was it a man or lady dressed like an elephant?

CHILD: It was a lady dressed like an elephant.

KELLEY: Was it a naked elephant did you say?

The interviewer's desire to hear about nakedness had clearly intervened here. But the quest had a way to go yet.

What was the elephant doing? the interviewer wanted to know.

CHILD: Just standing.

KELLEY: Oh, really. Were any of the private parts showing on the elephant?

The child could not say. Next came a string of questions about a bowl of ice cream and licking the bowl, which, the child maintained, was in the kitchen—a disconcerting answer.

KELLEY: But you said it was in the secret room with the elephant.

CHILD: No.

The interviewer proceeded to ask the girl if she had seen a penis on the elephant.

"He just has a tail," came the answer.

KELLEY: Did you ever see ice cream on the tail of the elephant?

CHILD: No.

Some children understood quickly that there was something to be gained by giving the interviewer what she asked for and soon began trading. One child had been permitted to telephone the automated weather report at the first interview and wanted to do so again at the second one. If she told "something special," she asked the interviewer, would she be allowed to call the weatherman? She would be allowed to do so, Nurse Kelley answered the child, but only by telling.

———

Gerald's trial, separated from that of his mother and sister, began in April 1986, nearly two years after the first accusations. In that time, the children who would serve as witnesses had been selected and prepared, their testimony having been developed in the course of the long interviews, mostly with Nurse Kelley. Persistence had yielded a wealth of charges, some inextricably entangled in stories and allusions the prosecutors would doubtless have preferred not to be broadcast from the mouths of their chief witnesses. Those stories told much about the processes that finally led the children to tell about bad things that Gerald, Miss Vi, and Cheryl had done.

Confronted with challenges to do as well as their friends who had told things, and with assurances that telling would make their parents proud and happy, the children in due course came up with things to tell. One boy who would become a witness for the prosecution maintained for three months that nothing had happened at Fells Acres, during which time his parents and interviewers queried him repeatedly. Finally he informed his therapist that balls of light and blue dots chased him at Fells Acres and that "16 kids have died from that school."

That these stories were a kind that would normally have caused an examiner to harbor the gravest doubts about the witnesses' credibility was of no particular consequence to the prosecutors. In cases like Fells Acres, in the era of the great mass abuse trials, investigators were not often hampered by worries about the capacities of the prosecution witnesses. The important thing, the Fells Acres prosecutors knew, was to get the witnesses on the stand and that those witnesses were children—children who would tell the jury about the sexual assaults Violet, Cheryl, and Gerald Amirault had made on them.

They knew that whatever happened on the stand, the jury would make allowances: the witnesses were innocent children. In this as in other cases around the country, prosecutors underscored this fact by seeing to it that the witnesses carried large teddy bears when they took the stand.

The witnesses against the Amiraults now were between six and eight and a half years old and had strange stories to tell. It was arranged that the children be seated in such a way that they didn't have to look into the faces of those they accused and be frightened.

One boy who gave testimony at Gerald's trial said that he had been tied naked to a tree outside the school. The teachers had killed animals. They had given the children white pills to make them go to sleep. Something bad had happened to a dog's leg. Under cross-examination, the child provided detail on the dog.

Q: What happened to his leg?

A: Vi and Cheryl took it off.

Q: How did they take his leg off?

A: With a knife.

The child also testified about the robot at Fells Acres. What did the robot look like? he was asked.

"An ordinary robot."

At Gerald Amirault's trial, a girl testified that he had jammed a knife into her rectum and been unable to get it out. A teacher the child named as "Miss Ann Marie" called out to ask what was going on. According to the witness, Gerald told her what he did with the knife.

"Don't do it again," Miss Ann Marie warned him.

This witness too had testimony to give about a robot at the school—one who had bitten her arm and warned children not to talk. Under cross-examination, she gave further details.

Q: What color was the robot?

A: Silver.

Q: Silver. Did it have lights on it?

A: Yes.

Q: And was it a big robot or was it a little robot?

A: Big.

The picture of the robot as it finally emerged was of a green, yellow, and silver creature with lights, which moved on wheels. The witness agreed, further, that the robot was someone like R2-D2 from *Star Wars*.

On the basis of her testimony, Gerald Amirault was convicted of raping the child with the knife he had so much difficulty removing and of indecent assault and battery.

Jennifer, the child who had so adamantly told Nurse Kelley she had not been touched, emerged as a witness at Gerald's trial. He was the bad clown, she told the court, and he took her to the magic room. There he put a pencil in her vagina and also touched her vagina.

This was a child much changed from the one seen in the initial interviews with Nurse Kelley, and not only because she was older. By the time of the trial, she had taken part in months of group therapy sessions where she and another former Fells Acres child played with anatomical dolls and exchanged stories about the school. One month after she began the therapy sessions, the child announced, according to her mother, that Miss Cheryl had taken pictures of the children without their clothes on.

An ever-present motif, the children's references to picture taking and cameras reflected the intense questioning of interviewers and prosecutors, concerned to establish the pornography motive. Everywhere in the accusatory testimony, Cheryl or Miss Vi or Gerald or one of the other teachers has a camera and is taking pictures.

The other teachers—other than the Amiraults, that is—figured large in the children's stories about Fells Acres. Twenty-two teachers and aides who had been employed at the school testified at the trials. None had ever seen anything amiss, or knew of secret rooms, children assaulted, or had seen Gerald in a clown suit.

The other teachers might have had reason to worry if the prosecution had been other than it was. As they became eager to tell about bad and scary things—as they were often told their classmates had already done—child after child named teachers other than the Amiraults as perpetrators. They offered abundant detail about how Miss Ann Marie or Miss Joanne or Miss Carol had hurt them, had taken pictures, been in the secret room. One girl declared at Gerald's trial that all of the teachers did "sex things" and were bad, except for "Miss Ann Marie." Another child witness referred to her teacher, Miss Ann Marie, though Miss Ann Marie was not in fact employed at the school at the time the girl attended.

The boy who testified at Gerald's trial that he had been tied naked to a tree said that all the Fells Acres teachers were there, and that all of them gave the children the white pills. In early interviews, he had reported that all the teachers took turns tying the naked children to the trees outside the school.

This information was of no apparent interest to the prosecutors, who ignored the naming of other teachers. The state had decided that the three Amiraults were the sole perpetrators and that the narrative they would present to the jury was of a family conspiracy. The conspiracy might well have included Cheryl's husband, Al, a name that began to appear in the stories children were offering the interviewer. A guy called Al punched them, a man called Al was there taking pictures and doing bad things. In the end, the prosecutors decided to leave the fortunate Al out of the indictment and concentrate on the family.

That the children had been questioned specifically about Al was clear, though the prosecutors were then and for years to come unshakeable in their position that the plaintiffs' accusations had been spontaneous and that the interviewers had made no suggestions that might have led the children to make them. Nurse Kelley, producer of most of the accusatory testimony against the Amiraults, left an extensive record of her interviews.

> KELLEY: How about when you were at Fells Acres? Did anyone touch your vagina?
>
> CHILD: No.

Nurse Kelley then went on to the next question, which was often the same question.

> KELLEY Oh. Did anyone at Fells Acres touch your vagina?
>
> CHILD: No. They took down our pictures.

The reference to pictures brought a new level of excitement to the exchange.

> KELLEY: What pictures?
>
> CHILD: From the walls.
>
> KELLEY: Who took your pictures at Fells Acres?
>
> CHILD: Not pictures of us—the pictures that we drew!
>
> KELLEY: Did anyone at Fells Acres take pictures of the girls with their clothing off?
>
> CHILD: No.

Middlesex County district attorney Scott A. Harshbarger, whose office prosecuted the Amiraults, had been a former public defender. Son of a Lutheran minister, he had attended Harvard, where he became a star football player, and went on to graduate from the university's law school. Early in his career as DA, some thought they detected in Harshbarger a touch of the thoughtful liberal—a touch that coexisted with a pronounced streak of rigidity.

Lawyers and judges present for the occasion still recall the uproar that took place at a legal conference in the late 1980s when someone asked panelist Harshbarger a hypothetical question: What if someone asked to retain him as counsel and then confessed that he had committed a murder—the very crime for which another man was to be excecuted the following week? Would he reveal this exculpatory testimony to keep an innocent man from being executed? Harshbarger's answer left no doubt as to where he stood: he would not violate the attorney-client privilege. Not even to save a man from execution, aghast members of the audience wanted to know. That was not his business, Harshbarger maintained.

The chief trial prosecutor was Lawrence Hardoon, a skillful attorney in his mid-thirties who became, in effect, media representative for the prosecution. The press would find in him an invaluable and ever available source on all matters relating to the Amirault case—the investigations, the trials, the evidence.

It was through Hardoon that members of the press first learned of the prosecution's belief that the Amiraults were all surely involved in the child pornography business. Lacking any evidence for the charge despite their global search for pictures, they could not bring their charge in court. Nonetheless, Hardoon informed members of the press, the fact they hadn't found any such pictures didn't mean they didn't exist. In another interview, a rapt Hardoon told reporters how it had come to him that the Amiraults were pornographers—a moment's inspiration that explained everything. He had been searching for the motives for these frightful crimes against children, and then the answer finally came to him. There was, he marveled, something wondrous in how it had all come together in the miraculous workings of the mind, which could in an instant yield a revelation.

The entire Amirault family, and Patti's parents and relatives, came daily to the courtroom during the two and a half months of Gerald's trial. The chaos of their lives now was such that it provided a certain insulation for Gerald and Patti, who began to become accustomed to a pervasive sense of unreality. Each morning they woke up and got the Herald and the Globe, to read about more charges, interviews with the child victims' families, and more lists of symptoms of child abuse to watch for.

On July 8, 1986, Gerald's case went to the jury. The Amirault family and Phil and Mary McGonagle's were optimistic about the outcome, certain that the jurors would not credit stories like those the children had told. The family had the idea that the jurors would see through the prosecutors' and their witnesses. After his arrest, Gerald Amirault had taken and passed two lie detector tests. These were not admissible as evidence, as the family members knew, but the fact added to their sense that the jurors would inevitably come to the right conclusion.

Gerald had taken the stand at the trial and had, in their eyes, done well. An impassioned defense attorney had done his utmost to show that the children had been led to make charges and to point to the incredible nature of their testimony.

The prosecutors had an answer to that argument. Children terrorized daily by Violet, Gerald, and Cheryl had naturally resorted to fantasies as their means of insulating themselves from the horrors they endured. Only with the greatest effort had the children overcome their fears long enough to come forward to tell their stories, chief prosecutor Lawrence Hardoon told the jurors. It was up to them to decide whether the brave efforts of these children, who had suffered so much, had been made in vain, whether those children would come away branded as liars, whether their courage would be rewarded.

The length of time the jury stayed out nurtured the Ami-

raults' hopes—the longest jury deliberation in Massachusetts history. Still, when their decision came, on July 19,
Gerald Amirault stood convicted of crimes against nine
children—eight counts of rape and seven counts of indecent
assault and battery. He was immediately remanded to Cedar
Junction prison to await sentencing.

The number of counts against Gerald would have come
as no surprise to anyone acquainted with the pattern of child
abuse prosecutions of this kind. As the one male figure involved, he could not have expected to escape the role that
prosecutors invariably assigned the man in such cases: that
of the most culpable and dangerous perpetrator. Nor could
he have hoped to escape the kind of sentence that went with
that gender-determined role: Gerald received a sentence of
thirty to forty years and has been behind bars since 1986.

———

After the guilty verdict, twenty-nine-year-old Patricia Amirault left the courtroom supported by her father and spent
most of the next three days in a stupor. It was not possible to
grapple with the new realities of her life yet. A teacher in the
public school system—a job from which she had taken leave
in order to work at Fells Acres—she was now the family's
sole support. Those three days she wanted mostly to stay

asleep. She could not think yet about how it was going to be to live without her husband, whom she had known twenty-five years, to whom she had been married seven years, and with whom she had brought three children into the world.

Without hope, she and the family awaited the outcome of the motion for a new trial. As they expected, trial judge Elizabeth Dolan denied the motion a month after the conviction and the next day sentenced Gerald to thirty to forty years in prison. Gerald was transferred from Cedar Junction to the Norfolk prison, where he was immediately placed in protective custody. He entered the unit reserved for convicted sex offenders, a population considered in some danger of violence from other prisoners. In Gerald's case, known throughout the state, it was not an unlikely risk. His first days in the tough general population of Cedar Junction prison had been frightening enough. Athletic, outgoing, with numerous loyal friends even now, he had never known what it was to live in fear of other men. He had, of course, never been in prison before.

Grant Snowden

Grant Snowden had grown up wanting little else but to be a law officer, a goal that seemed out of the question for years. Nearly two inches short of the 5'9" minimum height requirement still in place at the time, he worked at other jobs, never relinquishing hope of joining the force. In his teens, he undertook every conceivable exercise he thought might stretch his height, all of them, needless to say, useless.

He married, fathered a child, dutifully supported his family, and thought, albeit with dimming hope, of a police career. He continued, nonetheless, to file applications at the Homestead (Florida) Police Station, until, one day, the answer was yes: he had somehow become tall enough, or in some other way desirable enough, to be admitted as a police trainee. Following graduation, he became an officer in the South Miami Police Department.

Granted a new life, he cared nothing now for the old, for any of his usual leisure pastimes. The job absorbed his every waking moment. He chose to work nights because that was the busy time, the period of the hottest action. Snowden made his arrests, then dealt with all the paperwork and procedures in the morning, all of which could keep him working long into the afternoon. He often got home with barely time to grab a quick meal and some sleep before heading off to the job again, a schedule that would have seemed grueling to a man less in love with his work.

His dedication and skills did not go unnoticed. He was cited and decorated, and in 1984, he won particular honors for capturing two rapists. Working the midnight shift one night, he noticed an old station wagon going by with a woman and two men in the front seat. Something in the woman's look troubled him; he followed the car and looked for a good reason to pull it over, which he finally found when the driver made an illegal turn. Inside, he found a terrified woman, the back seat stained with her blood. She had been raped and robbed by the men, who had forced their way into the car at a stoplight. For this arrest and rescue, Snowden was named South Miami's Officer of the Year and celebrated as a hero, his picture in the paper.

Within a year, the headlines over his picture would be of a very different kind. In June 1984, the parents of a three-year-old boy charged Snowden with a sexual offense against their child. Reports of such offenses were now daily media fare in Dade County, where State Attorney Janet Reno was building a career as a child advocate and prosecutor of sex crimes. (In Florida, the state attorney is the same as a district attorney.)

None of this boded well for Officer Snowden, charged in the wake of one of Reno's most sensational prosecutions, the Country Walk Day Care case, inspiration for countless press stories and consciousness raising about predators lurking in nursery schools. All South Florida was agog, hot lines deluged with tips about likely predators and calls from panicked parents. In one week, state officials closed down eleven Dade County nursery schools as word spread about dozens of others under suspicion.

Grant Snowden's wife, Janice, had cared for Greg Wilkes since his infancy, as she had a hundred others in the fifteen years her home baby-sitting service was in operation. Never in those years had a parent complained, until the Snowdens noticed suspicious welts on the Wilkes child's face, bruises they had noticed more than once before, which had to have come, Grant concluded, from beatings.

He visited the boy's mother and father (also a police officer) to warn that he would make a report if he ever saw the child in such a condition again. Why he decided to stop at a mere warning without filing a report then and there, Officer Snowden could not later explain other than to say that it seemed the right thing to do.

That this would seem the right thing to do wasn't surprising in an officer whose citations praised his quiet handling of volatile situations. Thus encouraged, he became a believer in intercession and the art of "handling things." He thought his warning to the father would effect a change—a disastrous miscalculation.

Shortly after this encounter, the father charged that Snowden had committed an indecent act on his child—had put his mouth on the boy's penis. His son had reported it all, Greg's father declared. Shaken, the Snowdens were nonetheless certain, like others in their situation, that the allegation would soon be revealed as a lie, and everything would be cleared up. That certainty lasted roughly a day. Snowden was no man to sit calmly around waiting for a thing like this to resolve itself. He began his own incessant, nagging inquiries, going over the accusation again and again. He went so far as to visit the boy's parents, which effort ended in a scene: the accusing father insisted the story was true and began pressing his child to say the bad thing Grant had done to him—a failed effort, as it turned out. A therapist who later treated the child would note in her report that she had to warn the father to stop pressuring the boy to make charges.

Just days after the father's allegations, Snowden's superior informed him he was being investigated on charges of committing sexual battery on a minor. He was suspended from the force and instructed to show up at headquarters to surrender his gun and badge. Over his objections, Janice Snowden insisted on accompanying her husband to the station house. There he was immediately told to hand over his gun, which he did without much feeling. The badge was another matter. Told to hand it over, he felt a pain spread inside him, leaving him breathless.

Hearing nothing anyone said to him, he put the badge on the desk and left the station house, his anger mounting. He had been stripped of everything that mattered in the world. Had he filed a report on the child's father and been able to cite a record showing this motive for the charges, matters might have turned out otherwise. As it was, it was his word against an accuser charging him with assault on a child, a position whose grim possibilities he was only beginning to absorb. At the same time, he had lost none of his underlying confidence that the truth would emerge.

And in fact there was good news ahead. Lacking evidence to take to a grand jury, Reno's office decided not to press on with the father's charges. Snowden and his family rejoiced and began looking ahead, certain now that the trouble had been cleared up and that things would soon be back to normal.

In this they were mistaken, as they learned a few weeks later when Reno's office reopened the investigation. In the prevailing atmosphere, as the Snowdens did not yet know, there was no such thing as a truly discredited charge of child sex abuse. Lacking means to develop a case from the first complaint, the state attorney's office did what prosecutors bent on convictions were doing all over the country: they began to focus their inquiries on other children cared for at the Snowdens, whom they questioned at length. In time, they found an eleven-year-old girl who said she recalled being molested at the Snowdens at the age of four.

The case proceeded apace with the help of two authorities Janet Reno had heard were experts skilled in interrogating victims of abuse. Often presented to jurors as psychologists, Laurie Braga in fact had a Ph.D. in speech pathology; her husband, Joseph, had a doctorate in education. Taken with their reputations for expertise in child sex abuse, Reno decided to hire the Bragas for the Snowden case. Given quarters in the state prosecutors' offices, Laurie Braga began conducting interviews using dolls and "let's pretend" games and, as the interview records showed, exhortations and explicit sexual suggestions.

There was no mistaking the effectiveness of the testimony she produced—as central to this prosecution as nurse Susan Kelley's in the Amirault case.

Still, the prosecutors had their troubles. Notwithstanding the girl's rehearsals of testimony with Braga and with her own mother, the state could not overcome certain glaring problems in the eleven-year-old plaintiff's charges. Not least among these was the difficulty of convincing jurors that the child had been assaulted, as charged, on three consecutive days while at the Snowdens, when the evidence showed this could not have been so.

There before the jury were payment checks that the defense produced—checks that proved that the four year old had been sent elsewhere for baby-sitting during the entire span of months in which the attacks were supposed to have occurred. So improbable was the entire case that even in the reigning atmosphere, the jury came back with an acquittal.

The state was not unprepared for this outcome. The prosecutors would continue filing more and more new charges when the old proved unprofitable and keep introducing newly discovered victims. This they would do, they let Snowden know, because he was guilty and they knew it, and they would keep at it until he was convicted.

Even before the first trial ended in his acquittal, they told Snowden they would be filing new charges against him.

These were based on claims that he had assaulted a four-year-old girl taken to the Snowdens for baby-sitting. With each search for new victims, the prosecutors' witnesses became younger. It was evident that younger children would be more pliable, more endearing to jurors, and more difficult to resist.

Not only would the state charge Snowden with assault of a four year old; in the new trial held in 1986, they enlarged the victim list to include her eighteen-month-old brother.

The four year old provided testimony as planned, some of it more revealing than the state might have wished. She had visited with the prosecutors thirteen times, the child told the court proudly, and, she testified, she got "better and better" at telling her story. Nonetheless, the child clearly had no idea who Grant Snowden was and could not point him out in the courtroom.

At this trial, as at others like it, jurors presented with the children's accusations had no idea how they had been elicited and shaped. The four year old had repeatedly told her mother that Grant had not touched her. She told the interviewer that she wanted to live at the Snowdens and that she had asked her mother for permission to do so. This appeared to have little effect on the mother, who had become, like many involved in these trials, instantly and profoundly caught up in the drama of the prosecution, her role in it, and that of her child. Despite the girl's denials, she remained steadfastly invested in the prosecutor's case.

Page after page of Laurie Braga's initial interrogations revealed a child with nothing whatsoever to say about sex, though, as she told the interviewer, she knew from watching television that Grant had done bad things. She also revealed that her mother had instructed her to talk about Grant and to say that he had touched her—and where.

Nonetheless, the child clearly had other matters on her mind, though it did from time to time seem that she was about to make some telling disclosure.

INTERROGATOR: You were watching TV and then what would happen?

CHILD: And then Grant came up . . .

INTERROGATOR: Uh-huh?

CHILD: And shut off the TV.

What did Grant do then? Did he sit and play with her? the interviewer asked. He did nothing, the child informed her, and he had turned off the TV "because he can't sleep." And this had upset her, the child said. Again and again, the girl returned to the same vital matter—one thing that she herself had experienced, that no one had suggested to her or caused her to recite or imagine through make-believe doll games. Namely, that Grant had turned off the TV set.

With numerous variations of "You know what happened? Grant, when I was watching TV, he turned off the TV and I cried, " and no indication the child would ever mention sex abuse, Ms. Braga took matters in hand. She now offered the child, who had repeatedly said earlier that Grant Snowden had done nothing to her, choices from a rich list of sexual activities acted out on a doll.

"Did he rub his penis outside or put it inside . . . did he put his penis here or did he put his penis here or did he put his penis in your mouth? Where else?"

In all the possibilities offered the four year old, one option was notably absent—the choice, that is, that nothing sexual had happened.

Whatever the prosecutors' earlier difficulties building a case against Snowden, it was clear in the second trial that the hard times were over. The state could hardly have asked for bench rulings more helpful than those handed down by trial judge Amy Donner. In pretrial motions, she acceded to the state's request to bar any mention of Snowden's first trial and acquittal. Nor was the jury allowed to hear anything about Snowden's model career as a police officer.

The prosecutors were allowed to present testimony from two children having nothing to do with the case at hand.

One of these, brought forth to testify to "prior bad acts," was the boy, now four years old, whose facial welts had caused Snowden to warn the parents who had made the first accusation—an accusation the state had declined to send to the grand jury for lack of evidence. The other witness was a six-year-old girl Grant Snowden had never met. She gave testimony, nonetheless, having been interviewed at length by Laurie Braga, and she was the likely star witness at a new trial in the event the prosecutors again failed to win a conviction against Snowden.

In the crucial area of physical evidence—and nothing was more important to jurors than such evidence—the prosecutors offered Dr. Dorothy Hicks, who testified regularly for the state. According to this expert witness, director of Jackson Memorial Hospital's rape trauma treatment center, the four-year-old plaintiff had contracted a venereal disease—gardnerella vaginitis, a common infection also transmitted through nonsexual contact.

Whether the child in fact had such a condition, no one would ever know because the state's expert had destroyed the test-slide evidence. Dr. Hicks had tested for the disease using a sample of vaginal discharge from the child—a discharge, according to the child's parent, present in the girl two years before she had ever met the Snowdens. The jury was given to understand, nonetheless, that they been given the most authoritative possible evidence that Snowden was guilty, and they would hear no contradiction of the expert who had given it.

No defense rebuttal was to be permitted thanks to the judge's ruling barring the defense expert from giving testimony. The witness in question, Max Bertholf, was associate director of residency at Roanoke Memorial Hospital and a specialist in research on the diagnosis of sexually transmitted diseases. Laurie Braga, with no credentials as a child psychologist but a reputation as a child advocate and a doctorate in speech, had been permitted to present herself to the jury as an expert in child development. But when it came to Dr. Bertholf, Judge Amy Lee Donner ruled that he was not qualified to testify because he was not, the judge declared, an expert in the diagnosis of sexually transmitted diseases in children. That this medical specialty does not in fact exist did not dissuade Judge Donner. The procedures for diagnosing such diseases are the same for children as for adults, Dr. Bertholf informed the judge—in vain. The judge knew what she knew.

As a result, jurors would not be allowed to hear the defense expert testify to the notorious unreliability of the diagnostic test Dr. Hicks had used—a test that, according to Dr. Bertholf, yielded inaccurate results at least 50 percent of the time.

The state prosecutor began his summation with the announcement, "We are here because this man raped two kids." It continued with a recital of crimes never alleged against Snowden. The child, he assured jurors, "wouldn't talk about the anal rape . . . because those things are more horrible for a four-year-old to talk about than a finger." Snowden had never been accused of such a thing. The state was nonetheless allowed to leave jurors with the impression he had committed anal rape and violated the children in other ways more terrible than they had been allowed to know.

Grant Snowden was convicted in March 1986 after a two-week trial. His bond revoked immediately, he was taken into custody after being granted a few minutes to say goodbye to his grief-wracked family. At his sentencing in April, Judge Donner was moved to deliver a lesson of sorts suitable to the occasion. Before passing sentence, she read aloud an essay by a child abuse investigator who had stumbled on the truth that crimes against children were a great evil.

Snowden's statement was briefer. "You are fixing to sentence an innocent man," he told the judge, when asked if he wished to speak. Judge Donner proceeded to sentence Snowden, now thirty-nine, to five life terms. Under the circumstances, State Attorney Reno and prosecutors were content to drop their latest new charges.

Three months later, Snowden was taken from the county jail to begin serving his life terms. His route through the system began with the eight-hour journey to the reception center in Lake Butler. In the decade since, certain memories remain ever clear to him—among them, those of this trip in which he sat looking through the van's rear window for a last sight of home.

At Butler, where he was assigned to protective custody—he was not only a convicted child molester but a former police officer—he was told to take his clothes off and sent to his isolation cell. He got there walking naked down a long hallway carrying a box with all his possessions. There he waited until he was given his inmate uniform.

His odyssey through the Florida prison system began with a term at Cross City Correctional. From there, Snowden was transferred to Belle Glades, deep in the sugarcane fields, where he became an expert in killing the rats that infested the place. The moves to various prisons came without warning, and always in the middle of the night.

Shortly after he was sentenced, Snowden told his wife to divorce him, but Janice Snowden refused. After Grant's first appeal failed, he insisted, until finally Janice filed for divorce. Now certain he would remain in prison for life, he would entertain no hope nor could he deal with connections to the world outside—the anguish of his mother, brothers, and sisters. His bitterness and depression made it impossible for him to sustain conversations with them, as the family discovered. They could not get him to telephone them. On the occasions he chose to call, he advised his brothers and sisters, everyone, that they should simply go on with their lives and get used to the idea that his life was now prison.

He heard that Janet Reno had been appointed attorney general of the United States, news he barely noticed. Snowden's days were now exclusively concerned with the realities of life in prison—the here and now, the dangers, glimmerings of hope, the unknowable darkness of the years ahead. One day he encountered one of the rapists he had arrested, now serving fifteen years. The man recognized him at once and informed Snowden that he knew who he was, and held nothing against him—he was just a cop doing his job.

Snowden was relieved to hear it. He wanted no conflict, no battles, least of all those that had to do with who and what he had once been: an honored member of the force. A history dead and buried.

His injunction to his family—that they should simply go on with their lives—was of course impossible to obey. Grant Snowden was one of six children born to a struggling mother—children who had brought one another up in a hardscrabble early life, who had watched over each other and forged inseparable bonds.

Shortly after Grant was taken off to prison, his grief-maddened brother Terry took a plane to New York, a city in which he had never before set foot. Impelled by a force barely comprehensible to him, the thirty-five-year-old Floridian wandered the midtown streets until he found the CBS building. Somehow he managed to make his way to the CBS cafeteria, where he found someone from *60 Minutes*— exactly who he was looking for. Descending on correspondent Ed Bradley, he babbled the rough details of the story, offering to deliver any documents and proof needed. Nothing would come of this encounter, Terry quickly learned, as nothing would come of any lawyers' efforts over the decade ahead.

The Amiraults, Part Two

Cheryl's and Violet's trials had been severed from Gerald's at the request of the prosecutors, who argued that it would be hard on the children to have to testify against all three defendants at once. As the June 1987 trial approached, roughly a year after Gerald's had begun, the Amiraults and friends were no longer so optimistic, though they thought it possible that Violet's age—sixty-three—and her gender might make a difference in the prosecutors' capacity to persuade the jurors. It was a slim hope, as they knew. Upbeat as Patti, the Mc-Gonagles, and assorted relatives and friends always appeared, whether with one another or in public, most of them understood after Gerald's conviction that there was only one way this trial could come out.

A child who had not testified at Gerald's trial appeared at

this one to say that Cheryl, Violet, and Gerald had all taken her to the magic room. There she had to take her clothes off while Cheryl took pictures. The camera was tall with long feet, and it had three legs. Cheryl and Violet put a purple and white magic wand inside her vagina and anus. Cheryl and Violet put their mouths on her vagina.

The boy who testified at Gerald's trial about the dog's leg and the robot told the court now that Violet had pushed a stick up his anus and that Cheryl put her mouth on his penis. Cheryl warned him that if he told his parents, they would be killed.

Unlike Gerald, Violet and Cheryl did not take the stand, a fact that the state prosecutors often cited as an indicator of their guilt. Their attorney made the decision after concluding that the tranquilizers they were taking made them seem dazed and would damage their capacity to defend themselves under hard cross-examination.

The state's last witness had nothing to say directly about the Amiraults, strangers to him as he to them. Unable to introduce charges of child pornography, for which they had no evidence of any kind, the prosecutors decided they would bring a witness to raise the matter by implication, which they were allowed to do without objection from the bench. Thus did a postal inspector Dunn take the stand to regale jurors with a commentary on the evils of child pornography.

On June 12, their case went to the jury. This time, the deliberations were brief. The next day the jury came in with a verdict finding Violet and Cheryl guilty on all counts.

The next day, to the astonishment of her supervisors at United Parcel Service, Cheryl showed up for work as usual. She had held a job there for three years, since Violet's school closed. When she got the job in November 1984, the Amirault name and that of Fells Acres were already notorious. Somehow, in the effort to find workers for the Christmas rush ahead, Cheryl went unrecognized. Not till the three Amiraults were indicted a few months later, their pictures in all the papers and on television, did anyone at United Parcel Service figure out who she was. By that time, she had established herself as an immensely industrious employee and had won friends. Her supervisors saw no reason to get rid of her—a person they felt they knew.

For nearly three years, she had juggled the demands of her situation and the job, and she had managed. She took half-days when pretrial requirements demanded it and UPS vacation days for the trial.

She had no hesitation going to work the day after the verdict, nor did she give the matter any thought. She dressed; she went. In the job she had found a form of tranquilizer more potent than any a pharmacy could provide. It is not surprising that she should have tried to hold on as long as possible to that proof of membership in respectable society. On that June day, nevertheless, her supervisor had to tell her the job was over. There was now a guilty verdict. Cheryl tried to argue that there would be an appeal, to no avail, as the supervisor sorrowfully shook his head.

Two months of freedom remained. In July, Judge John Paul Sullivan sentenced Violet and Cheryl to a term of eight to twenty years.

In August, the two entered the Women's Correctional Facility at Framingham. Processed and handed their state clothes, they spent the first night in a cage-like enclosure, separated from the rest of the prison population. On the plastic mattress issued them, Violet sat holding her trembling daughter. Years later, Cheryl still wondered at her mother's composure that day. Curled up in Violet's arms with a blinding headache (all medications had been taken from them), Cheryl cringed at the sight of the insects speeding across the floor. There were roaches, she announced. Violet told her daughter not to worry; a lot of people had roaches and got used to them.

In the morning, someone slid a bowl of oatmeal through the cage, their breakfast. From time to time, an inmate would walk past the cage and hurl curses at the child molesters. The night before their arrival, the entire population of the women's prison had been called to an assembly and told that the Amiraults were arriving the next day and that there would be a general lockdown. Everyone would be confined to their cells that night. The women were warned that any disturbance of the peace or misbehavior directed at the Amiraults would bring severe disciplinary measures.

The inmates were furious that they would be confined to their cells because these two had arrived, and they were above all angry at the Amiraults for who they were. Violet and Cheryl left the cage only for meals, served by inmates who expressed their view of the women by issuing the scantiest of portions and glaring at them. When Violet and Cheryl sat down at a table, everybody sitting there would get up and leave. Women cursed at them.

The Amirault women spent three weeks assigned to the cage before moving on. The authorities initially wanted to put them in maximum security for their own safety, but Violet balked. "You put us in here; you take care of us," she told a supervisor. At the end of the three weeks, the prison officials agreed to allow them to enter the general population.

The day they entered their unit, every inmate was out on the grounds to watch. Once settled, Violet and Cheryl met with a supervisor who offered advice. It was important that they go to every meal without fail, she told them. They should not stay in their cell, but rather should walk the grounds every day. The idea, she told them, was to let the other inmates get the hostility out of their systems.

There was plenty of that, Violet and Cheryl found; catcalls followed them everywhere. Wherever they walked on the grounds, eight to ten guards marched behind them. For a while, the Amirault women thought this might be the process for all new inmates. But it soon dawned on Violet, after days of hearing catcalls about the guards, that this was far from the case—that she and Cheryl were receiving special treatment, which only enraged the other inmates.

At Violet's request, the guards were removed. This produced no immediate lessening of hostility from the other women—they still got up to leave when Violet and Cheryl sat down at a dining room table—but the catcalls about special guards stopped. Gradually Violet and Cheryl began to receive overtures of friendship, most of them in the form of food offerings. Would Violet or Cheryl like her extra egg? one would ask. Another would offer something else in the way of extra food.

Food was no small issue in prison, particularly breakfast, and particularly for Violet, who required daily blood pressure and heart medication. Each morning throughout her years at Framingham, the choice was whether to stand in the chow line for breakfast or the line for medication. Time was limited because all units had to be fed at the same time in the morning. Violet chose medication, raced to the dining hall for coffee, and back to her cell for the first count of the day. In time, the prison authorities pushed the first of the daily counts, of which there were thirteen, up to midmorning.

Improvements like this did not impress Violet, whose certitude about how things should and should not be done did not abandon her at Framingham. That she was a prisoner of the state, an outcast even in prison society, charged with unspeakable crimes, did not alter her faith in her own good judgment. In the midst of her shock at being cast into prison, and her grief, which she tried to conceal from Cheryl, Violet recorded everything that was wrong with the way the prison was run. For a caller speaking to her from the outside, it was not unusual to hear, between alternating currents of anger and hopelessness, calmly recited details of the prison operations and the ways it could be made more efficient.

Noting her age and responding perhaps to her air of authority, a number of the women inmates began to call her "mama," a term an angry Cheryl did not want attached to her mother under these circumstances. She could not be seen as the mother of people like these, she told Violet. She was not a criminal; the Amiraults were not criminals.

Though none of the Amiraults were churchgoers prior to their prosecution, Cheryl now found comfort in prayer and became a faithful attendant at all the services, Protestant, Jewish, and Catholic, but Violet would have none of it. When it came to religion now, Violet was unpersuadable, wanted nothing to do with churches or prayers. If there was a God, he had abandoned them, allowed their lives and all she had worked for, all she had earned, to be destroyed.

The only thing left to her was a house, now occupied by her new husband. Just before she was imprisoned, she had married the man she had been seeing—a tall, dapper salesman who spent a good deal of time on the road. She married Bob not only because she cared for him but also to ensure that there would be someone on the outside bound to her, who could be depended on. Though Violet in time suspected she had made a miscalculation about Bob, it was still a comfort to know he was there.

In the press, the Amiraults' story was over, the reporters having gone on to other things. One day in their first year behind bars, Violet and Cheryl spotted a tour group of state officials and accompanying journalists. One of them was a reporter ever at their door from the investigations to the jury verdict, a kindly man eager to hear all the Amiraults had to say. From their corner of the prison Violet and Cheryl screamed his name—"Charlie! Charlie!" They screamed until he turned and saw them, and turned away.

———

A few months after the second Amirault trial ended, the prosecutors sponsored a seminar titled "The Fells Acres Day

School Case—A Model Multidisciplinary Response." At this meeting, chaired by District Attorney Scott Harshbarger, social service workers, therapists, and other state witnesses paid tribute to all who had brought the case to its fruition. The speakers included co-prosecutor Patricia Bernstein, who expressed gratitude that a sensitive and creative judge had allowed the child witnesses to sit so that they did not have to face the accused. Other speakers pondered problems this model case illustrated. Some of the Fells Acres parents had, for example, refused to believe the charges—parents in denial, as they were described.

A speaker next addressed the physical evidence of abuse. Although the prosecutors had offered none that could be counted as such, they did have expert witnesses to provide support for some of the more remarkable of the children's accusations. One of these was Dr. Jean Emans, who gave testimony with regard to a child's claim that Gerald had penetrated her anally with a knife. In court the doctor testified that an object could "touch the hymen on the way to trying to find the anus" without penetrating the vagina. The object was in this instance a butcher knife—an item that had presumably managed to work its way through delicate tissues without injury or any signs thereof. Who were the jurors to think they knew better than an expert? The jurors had, moreover, been instructed in the special skills of child abusers—

molesters whose cunning could make all sorts of things possible.

The parents were no less respectful of the experts who told them their children had been tortured and raped. Educated by the investigators, the Fells Acres parents quickly accepted that their children had daily suffered the cruelest of assaults and terrors, whose effects they had simply lacked the expertise to notice. For parents so educated, it was now plausible that their children had been stabbed, raped with sticks, that they been forced to watch animal mutilation and to drink urine, and be threatened with death for two years—and that they nonetheless continued to go happily off to the school every morning and show no fear of their torturers. Just after the allegations about the Amiraults and Fells Acres became public, the Boston papers were packed with quotes from parents telling of their children's love of the school and of the worry the children expressed that they wouldn't be able to go to Fells Acres anymore.

———

When Violet and Cheryl entered the Framingham prison, Gerald had already been in prison a year and was by then well educated in all that it meant there to carry the label of child molester. In the prison social order, the top ranking belongs to killers of police officers. The child abuser occupies the lowest rung but one—the place reserved for the killer of a child.

Walpole, where Gerald was sent for two days' processing, was home to some of the hardest-core criminals in the state, all of them well acquainted with the crimes charged to the Amiraults. So were all the prison personnel, who told one another, when the prisoner arrived, "Take him to the magic room." That night the prison shook with the noise of inmates banging on the bars of the cells chanting, "Hang it up, Tooky!"

His processing completed, Gerald was sent to Norfolk prison's protective custody unit, where it was brought home to him that protective custody could not entirely protect him. This he learned shortly after his arrival, when a fist came smashing into his face as he walked behind a guard escorting him to his unit. It took some time for life in Norfolk to improve, which it did decidedly when the other prisoners turned their attention to a new arrival, a man convicted of killing two children.

The sucker punch that broke his nose and landed him in the Norfolk prison hospital was not his first encounter with violence or the worst. Shortly after he was accused in 1984, someone had fired into the house, barely missing the crib where Gerald and Patti's newborn son lay sleeping. They discovered the identity of the shooter when Patti's father, Phil, who knew everyone in town, made inquiries. As the family suspected, the gun had been fired by a parent of one of the Fells Acres children.

When the state sent Gerald Amirault to prison, he left behind three children of his own—daughters Gerrilyn, aged six, and Katie, aged seven, and a son, P.J., twenty-two months. The family now began a new existence revolving largely around the absent Gerald, a tumultuous life of work, prison visits, and a daily schedule of phone calls so the children could talk to their father. When Gerald was taken away, Patti prepared to deal with the next worst moment, which was telling the children. A teacher practiced in work with the young, it was nevertheless impossible for her to imagine that she could find a way to explain to her own why their greatly adored father would not be coming home. The children's strong attachment to him was obvious early. Wherever Gerald was, there the children were sure to be. When year-old Katie had trouble sleeping, he would be the one to sit up rocking her.

"Try letting her cry," her mother would urge when the child woke for the fifth time, directions Gerald invariably refused.

When he was brought to trial, the girls were just old enough to grasp that a great trouble had come to the family. Their father, grandmother, and Cheryl were in court, their pictures on television, because, it was explained, some people claimed that they had done bad things to children, but those people were wrong. The boy, named P.J., knew nothing and would, unlike the girls, retain no memory of his father at home. He would certainly not remember, though his mother did, the hide-and-seek game Gerald played with the boy, in whose finale Gerald always tiptoed upstairs and into the bedroom, where, to the child's noisy delight, his father swept him up in a great hug. Months after Gerald had been taken away, his wife hated to go up the stairs for fear the floorboard would creak, a sound P.J. associated with his father and their game. Every time he heard it, the child began calling "Da!" expecting, evidently, his father would soon enter the room.

When the trials ended and the TV cameras were gone, when the district attorneys had finished celebrating their model prosecution and no one talked about Fells Acres anymore, the Amiraults were left holding on to one another and their lives. They lived, brought up the children, celebrated holidays and christenings and hope when they could find it. When the time came for the children's First Communion, the girls wore their white dresses to the prison and P.J. his suit, so their father could see them and in this way take part.

To make ends meet, Patti Amirault worked three jobs, supplementing her teacher's salary with what she earned clerking at Filene's and another part-time position servicing ATM machines. On weekends, she took the children to the prison to visit Gerald. Early in his term, he was transferred to Billerica Prison, an ancient place lacking climate control and numerous other modern comforts but offering one crucial advantage: it was close enough to home so that the family could visit a few times a week, and there were no glass walls, as there would be in the next penitentiary, to prevent contact with visitors.

In their different ways, Gerald's children accommodated themselves to the new life, which included weekly visits to his prison and nightly phone calls, eagerly awaited, in which they could tell him everything that happened at school. For P.J., there was nothing new or strange about any of it. Unlike his sisters, who were angry and tearful when they left their father at the end of visiting day, he had no experience of Gerald other than this. His father was a man in an orange jumpsuit and had always been.

For Gerald, life now was the telephone. With it, he listened, advised, and tried to absorb what he could not share. He wanted every detail. He heard about picnics, outings, birthday parties, and he could coach his son, who shared Gerald's mania for sports, in baseball or hockey. His father-in-law, Phil, or one of Patti's brothers attended P.J.'s games and reported to Gerald. That way, if his son had problems in technique, Gerald could advise him, and if the boy did well, he could know the particulars. Through the nightly calls, he could make clear his disappointment if his daughters or his son fell short at school, as he could his pride and happiness that they were his children.

The children accustomed themselves to everything except daily traffic in a society that viewed their father as a monstrous criminal and tormentor of children. One day during Gerald's first year in prison, the seven-year-old Gerrilyn decided she wanted to send her father some of her drawings. She spent only a moment inside the post office before she came rushing outside, where her mother was waiting. Crying bitterly, the girl related that when she gave the envelope to the postal clerk, he stopped and looked at it. "Why do you want to write to this horrible man?" the clerk wanted to know.

"He's my father," the child answered.

Her enraged mother raced into the building, found the man, and delivered a scathing piece of instruction on what was and was not the business of a postal clerk. The next day she dispatched a letter to the postmaster general, who answered, with surprising promptness, that he was sincerely sorry and that the clerk had been disciplined. Even so, Patti worried about the effects of such an experience on her daughter—worries not entirely unjustified. For some time after, Gerrilyn did not enter a store or go anywhere else without a certain apprehension about what some stranger might say to her. She had no apprehensions about school, where everyone knew who the Amiraults were and no one ever mentioned her father.

In March 1989, the Supreme Judicial Court of Massachusetts unanimously denied Gerald's appeal for a new trial. A year later, the court rejected Violet and Cheryl's appeal. The ruling came with a stinging dissent from Justice Paul Liacos, arguing that the conviction should have been overturned because the trial judge had allowed the prosecutor to introduce postal inspector Dunn's reflections on child pornography. Of his colleagues' denial of the appeal, Justice Liacos said, "The court today condones the admission in evidence of highly inflammatory and prejudicial evidence." Clearly, the justice charged, the commonwealth wanted the jury to infer that because pornographers having no connection with the defendants took pictures of children, so had the Amiraults.

Violet and Cheryl came up for parole in 1992. At the end of their trial, prosecutor Hardoon had described the Amiraults as impudent for their refusal to acknowledge their guilt—a refusal, he charged, that only compounded the injury done to the children and their families. It would not be the last time the state expressed its views on this matter. In

1992, after five and a half years in prison, Violet and Cheryl's applications for parole were denied on the grounds that they continued to maintain their innocence.

"Parole denied, " the board report on Violet concluded. "Vigorously denies the offenses. Until such time as she is able to take responsibility for her crimes and engages in long-term therapy to address the causative factors she will remain at risk to the community if released." The report on Cheryl concluded similarly, citing "heinous crimes for which she takes no responsibility."

Learning of this outcome, superior court judge John Paul Sullivan came to a conclusion of his own. The judge, who had presided over the women's trial, had long harbored doubts, albeit quietly, about the truth of the charges against the Amiraults. The reason Violet and Cheryl were denied parole had only strengthened his concerns. In prison for over five years, the women had been willing to sacrifice their chance to go free rather than make a confession. It was a telling fact, not to be ignored, and it had a profound effect on Judge Sullivan, now assailed by a certainty that Violet and Cheryl neither could or would ever make a confession. This meant they could well end up serving a full twenty-year term.

After their parole was denied, their attorneys applied to the trial judge for a revision of the women's sentence. Judge Sullivan did not hesitate to grant the revise-and-revoke order resentencing them to time served. When passing the original sentence, declared the judge, he had never intended Violet and Cheryl to serve more than five years.

In no way prepared to accept early release for any of the Amiraults, the Middlesex County District Attorney's office went into combat mode. The Amiraults' chief trial prosecutor, Lawrence Hardoon, by now in private practice, raced to the Supreme Judicial Court with a brief opposing the women's release, which the justices granted. The court decision overturning Judge Sullivan's order was technically correct. Judge Sullivan's argument for revising the sentence—that he had intended that they should serve only five or six years and now they had been denied parole—ran afoul of the prohibition against making changes on the basis of factors that took place after the original sentencing.

All unaware Violet and Cheryl said their goodbyes and prepared to go home, laden with boxes of their accumulated belongings. They had been moved to Lancaster prison for their prerelease period. Thankful to be freed, the women made excited plans. Outside, a car packed with family members awaited them. Then, in the midst of the preparations and the chatter, Cheryl was summoned to a supervisor, who offered apologies: she and her mother were not to be released after all, she told Cheryl. There had been a mistake in reading the court order. And she was worried, the supervisor said, about the effect this news would have on Violet.

The supervisor was not thinking of Violet's physical condition. Composed though she might be during the day, Violet screamed through the nights, beset by hellish dreams. A prison doctor diagnosed night terrors, which beset her, despite medication, nearly every night in prison.

The supervisor's fears notwithstanding, Violet suffered no particular ill effects from this event. Her combative instincts now emerged full force, directed mainly at her attorneys and filling her with abundant energy as she contemplated everything that had gone wrong from the trial on down to this day. If the attorneys had been devoted, Violet also had the feeling they had not been up to the job—that she herself could have made better arguments than they did.

Still, how many lawyers were up to the job of defending clients like these? It was a question. Judge Sullivan recalled the atmosphere of the times and the statistics. "You can see that there were *no* acquittals in cases of this kind—involving children—for years."

Around the same time Violet and Cheryl were denied parole in 1992, former prosecutor Lawrence Hardoon instructed a Boston Globe interviewer in the reasons the war on child abuse was so urgent—more urgent, he suggested, than the requirement that everyone accused be guilty as charged. Should not society, he asked, be "willing to trade off a couple of situations that are really unfair, in exchange for being sure that hundreds of children are protected?" It was not a comment that would have made many readers blink. After two long and sensational prosecutions focusing on the allegedly barbarous practices of child abusers like the Amiraults, the public was not disposed to doubt the authorities who put the criminals away.

Despised though they were as monsters by the public at large, Violet, Cheryl, and Gerald still commanded the loyalty of a circle of friends and neighbors who never believed the prosecutors' charges—people who visited the prison, helped with the Amirault children, and took up collections so that Gerald's wife could have a decent car. At the school where she taught fourth grade, Patti Amirault found unstinting support from colleagues and administrators. They, like everyone else, had heard about and read the horrific details of the Amiraults' crimes, and everyone had seen the television reports in which parents of the victim children appeared. Invariably disguised in wigs and glasses, their voices altered to conceal their identities, the parents spoke of the outrages their children had endured, the pain of their suffering that would afflict them the rest of their lives.

The Amiraults' friends, neighbors, and fellow teachers had heard all these things along with the rest of the public, and still none of it could persuade them that Violet, Gerald, or Cheryl had committed any such crimes. That they felt as they did had everything to do with the fact that the Amiraults were not strangers. The news reports could not alter the features of people so well known to their friends as Gerald was, or Cheryl and Violet were, or make them appear as monsters. It was not necessary to have been long-time friends of the three to feel this way. It was enough, perhaps, to see, up close, the daily struggles of a family member trying to vindicate them. Her colleagues knew Patti Amirault as a woman resolute and honest, unafraid to speak her mind. They were not likely to believe, if it ever occurred to them to think about the matter, that she would be married to a man guilty of the basest crimes against children or that she would fight with all her heart to free such a person. For Patti's fellow teachers it was enough to witness her hardship, her determination that the children not lose a single minute of possible connection with their father, to know which side they were on. The suffering they saw up close was the suffering they could believe.

———

In August 1995, Violet and Cheryl Amirault were released. Their attorneys had filed a motion for a new trial on grounds that the special seating arrangements at the trial allowing the Fells Acres children to avoid looking at the defendants violated the defendants' constitutional right to face their accusers. Normally a motion for a new trial would be granted by the trial judge, but John Paul Sullivan had retired. His replacement for this case was Robert Barton, son of a Boston physician who had served as a captain in the Marine Corps. Barton had a reputation as a fair but tough judge, known particularly for the long sentences he gave the deserving guilty. Appointed to the bench in 1978, the politically conservative Barton had developed something of a following. Attorneys called him Black Bart. In the state's prison population he was known as Boom Boom Barton because, as a prisoner fondly explained in a letter, he delivered a sentence with both barrels.

In 1985, while serving as sentencing judge in a carjacking case, Barton had confronted a convicted defendant who threatened he would come out and get him, the district attorney, and everyone else who had put him away. So, he told Barton, he had better not give him the fifteen years the district attorney recommended. He'd better give him life. Barton promptly gave the man a life sentence.

Well aware of Barton's reputation, Violet and Cheryl's new appellate attorneys, Daniel R. Williams and James L. Sultan, were not hopeful. Nor were they encouraged by the Amiraults' experience in the Massachusetts courts thus far.

They could scarcely have been more mistaken. Judge Barton announced his decision vacating the women's conviction in a Newburyport, Massachusetts, courtroom. An informed student of the case, he had, like Judge Sullivan, few doubts that the three Amiraults had been falsely prosecuted, the children manipulated into making accusations. The judge nonetheless now confined his ruling to the issue at hand: the right to confront one's accuser. Even more explicitly than the Sixth Amendment, the Massachusetts Declaration of Rights requires that the accuser face the accused. The Amirault women having been denied the right to confront their accusers, Judge Barton declared, their conviction was reversed.

In the stately courtroom jammed with television crews and reporters, all eyes focused on Violet and Cheryl brought from prison for the occasion, in leg chains and handcuffs. Clearly relishing the moment, Judge Barton spoke in slow and measured cadences. The time had come, he announced, to put an end to the injustice that had been done in this case. Violet and Cheryl Amirault must not spend another day, another hour, another minute in prison. It was to become the soundbite of the night, heard on every news program in Massachusetts.

Although Violet was free, Cheryl was not. A charge alleging an altercation with another inmate had to be cleared up before she could be discharged. Attorney James Sultan assured the family that this minor hitch would be cleared up in a day, but it was a day that required Cheryl's return to Framingham. As the car approached the prison, she saw that the entire inmate population had turned out on the grounds to greet her and roar in exultation at the judge's announcement.

Cheryl was freed the next day and did not regret the fact. Another day's confinement was little enough to pay for the chance to have witnessed the scene at the gates, the roars of joy that filled her ears and her heart. It was all a far cry from the reception the despised Amiraults had encountered when they entered prison eight years earlier. Once their guilt had been called into question in the outside world, their case taken up in the media—and nothing was more impressive or influential in the world of the prison than media attention—the other inmates had been won over. They now viewed Violet and Cheryl as innocent women—in a world of the guilty, innocence mattered—and exulted in the prospect of their redemption.

The reception Violet got upon her release lasted all day. Newburyport's largest and best bed-and-breakfast, a dignified, carefully maintained accommodation oozing with history, was overrun. To the astonishment of the inn's owners, newspaper and radio reporters, journalists and camera crews from every network began crowding through their door and were soon tramping around the back garden, where Violet

Amirault sat surrounded. The delighted owners, who had somehow managed to miss learning about the Amirault case up to now, welcomed the horde of media, worked themselves to exhaustion, and tried not to notice what was happening to the furniture, the rugs, or even the elegant upstairs bathroom, where a reporter had left a cigarette butt burning on the windowsill.

All morning, Violet held forth, not only about the case and her years in prison, but about politics, society, the world at large. She had led a sheltered life, she told the crowd around her, and had encountered in prison sights she had never seen before. She had never seen women withdrawing from heroin, cold turkey. It was a sight they should all see, she informed them.

Someone worried around midday that Violet might be getting too much of a sunburn. Waving a disparaging hand, she summoned the next reporter and turned her face up to the sun. The sun was good, Violet declared, good for everything. Every chance she got at Framingham, she sat broiling her face.

"You sit, you close your eyes, it was heaven, it was like feeling normal."

The attorneys and her family decided they should have a quiet lunch break with her, though there was nothing quiet in the reception the group found in the streets of the town. Passing truckers blasted their horns and gave her the thumbs-up sign, people leaned out of their car windows and called her name.

Yes, it was a happy day, Violet agreed, when someone asked. It would be much happier if she knew when her son would be released.

The days immediately following turned out not quite so happy. Returning to the house she shared with Bob, she found herself lost, confounded by certain changes he had made. Her husband had installed a new shower she had no idea how to use, and she could say the same about the fancy new telephones. None of this could account for the overwhelming sense of estrangement she felt looking around the place. She felt dispossessed, she told Cheryl the first day at home. Anxious and impatient, she waited for Bob to arrive for their first at-home reunion.

Finally he was there at the door, but instead of embracing her when she ran to him, he turned away. He had been seeing another woman while Violet was in prison—as she had suspected—and he was not about to stop now.

Embittering as this was, it could not match the desolation that overcame her when she again confronted the loss of her life's achievement—her school. She was now penniless; everything she owned had gone to pay the trial lawyers. And she and Cheryl were not yet out of danger. As the prosecutors made clear, they had every intention of overturning Judge Barton's ruling.

The Middlesex County prosecutors lost no time issuing word of their intent to see the women's conviction reinstated. They would do this, not least, District Attorney Tom Reilly announced, because the release of the convicted child molesters could only traumatize their victims and cause them more pain. Considered something of a zealot, particularly where headline-making cases were concerned, Reilly once explained himself to reporters. He knew something about suffering, he informed the Boston Globe in 1988. He had lost his father at an early age, and his brother had been killed by a car. That was the reason he could relate "to families and survivors having to deal with tragedy and how their lives never change." The Middlesex County district attorney clearly had in mind families like those who had been plaintiffs in the Amirault case.

Reilly's predecessor, Scott Harshbarger, who had brought the case against the Amiraults, had gone on to become attorney general of Massachusetts. When the questions about the case began making news in 1995, Attorney General Harshbarger argued that those raising questions about the Amiraults' guilt had abandoned the child victims. Moreover, to raise such questions was to expose the children and their families to further suffering. Expanding on his point, Harshbarger went on to compare the crimes of the Amiraults with those of serial murderer John Wayne Gacy, in whose house were found some twenty corpses. He saw as well a similarity between the Amiraults and child killer Joel Steinberg.

"Suddenly, " the Massachusetts attorney general told a group of Boston reporters, "we're branding these kids liars again."

Within a day of the women's release, parents of children in the Fells Acres case gave interviews. On television, in their customary wigs and other disguises, they told of their children's terror that Cheryl or Violet could come and get them.

Shortly after Violet and Cheryl's conviction was overturned, Gerald's attorneys filed a new trial motion. The ruling would have to come from Judge Elizabeth Dolan, who had presided over Gerald's trial. She had been praised as sensitive at the prosecutors' posttrial seminar, "A Model Multidisciplinary Response," and won similar plaudits for devising the special seating arrangements for the child witnesses.

Two years before Gerald's motion for a new trial, Judge Dolan had presided over another notable Massachusetts case—that of sixty-one-year-old Ray and Shirley Souza, whose twenty-four-year-old daughter had had a dream one night. In the dream, her parents raped her. It was now the 1990s, the era of the repressed memory syndrome. Ray and Shirley's grandchildren were taken to see therapists and interrogated. In court, they testified that their grandparents had tied them in a cage in the basement and then raped them with elbow and feet and a big machine. Judge Dolan decided that the children's testimony was credible and sentenced the Souzas (who had waived a jury trial) to a term of nine to fifteen years.

Gerald's attorneys were not optimistic about Judge Dolan's response to his appeal. Their feelings were well founded. In November 1995, the judge declared she could find no grounds for a new trial.

A year earlier, Gerald had been moved to a new prison, far more depressing than ancient Billerica, close to home, where he had spent eight years. The old place offered few amenities, but there, he could sit in the same room with his wife and children during visits. In the newly built climate-controlled Plymouth County Correctional Facility not far from Plymouth Harbor, visitors and inmate may talk only by phone though a glass wall. Here in a fifty-one-man unit securely separated from the general population, he lived in a doorless 12-by-12 cubicle with three other inmates. His was, to be sure, a bottom bunk, one of the perquisites of a senior prisoner. Here he spent much of the early morning reading, until it was time to begin making phone calls, the first among these going usually to the McGonagles. In the years since he was taken off to prison, no day passed that he didn't talk with Mary or Phil. The daily calls with Gerald could turn difficult immediately after an appeal was lost, when his hopes had been dashed. That, said his mother-in-law, Mary, who waited for his phone call every day, was when he needed to talk. "Somebody has to lift up his heart."

Gerald's heart and those of all the Amiraults and the McGonagles sorely needed uplifting in March 1997, when the Supreme Judicial Court of Massachusetts ruled for the prosecutors and reinstated the women's conviction. A year and a half after Judge Barton's ruling freed them, the court ordered Violet, now seventy-three, and Cheryl, thirty-nine, to be returned to prison. Immediately after the issuance of the decision, District Attorney Tom Reilly filed for the revocation of their bail.

The Supreme Judicial Court of Massachusetts, the oldest continuously sitting court in North America, had its beginnings in the era of the Salem witch trials. It was created to put an end to those trials and establish a rational system of justice. The court's decision in Violet and Cheryl's case was the work of Associate Justice Charles Fried, formerly Ronald Reagan's solicitor general. Fried prided himself on a career as a staunch judicial conservative. He viewed with antipathy any tendency to permit cases to stay open through multiple appeals, which he saw as a corruption of the legal process. The justice was nothing if not concerned with process. The members of the Supreme Judicial Court were awed and delighted when Fried, an esteemed intellectual and writer on the law, took leave from the Harvard Law School faculty to join them. All but one member of the court signed on to the justices' decision in the Amirault case—one that came to be remembered mainly for its argument on the importance of finality and that brought a flood of opposition from every political quarter, including judicial conservatives.

In a decision rich with rhetorical asides from Shakespeare and the Bible, Justice Fried acknowledged that a hysteria had affected the investigations of child abuse at the Fells Acres Day School. It was true, he affirmed, that the children had been subjected to leading questions and suggestions that led "to charges that might never have occurred to the children." Some of the children's testimony was highly improbable. Moreover, the decision found, the defendants' consitutional right to confront their accusers had indeed been violated. But in the opinion of the court, none of these factors raised a substantial risk of miscarriage of justice. Nor did they, as Justice Fried's decision explained, "awaken doubts" that warranted overturning the convictions. The complaints had already been fully aired at two trials. The juries had spoken. "The mere fact that if the process were redone there might be a different outcome, or that some lingering doubt about the first outcome may remain, cannot be a sufficient reason to reopen what society has a right to consider closed."

The course of justice must not be endless. Once the

process has run its course, the decision held, "the community's interest in finality comes to the fore."

Five other members of the Supreme Judicial Court of Massachusetts—Justices Margaret Marshall, Herbert Wilkins, Ruth Abrams, John Greaney, and Neil Lynch—signed on to this decision.

The lone dissenter, Justice Francis P. O'Connor, argued, significantly, that in these cases (he meant both Amirault trials) "the Commonwealth presented no scientific or physical evidence linking the defendants to the crimes" and that this was a case in which the jury had to make a verdict on the assessment of the child witnesses' credibility. The absence of face-to-face confrontation therefore was surely an error of consequence, weighty enough to suggest that without it, the trials' outcomes might have been otherwise.

"In both cases," Justice O'Connor argued, "a substantial risk of a miscarriage of justice has been established. Our desire for finality should not eclipse our concern that in our courts justice not miscarry."

The prosecutors expressed satisfaction that justice had been done. Attorney General Scott Harshbarger spoke of the innocent children who would finally be able to sleep at night. District Attorney Tom Reilly accused the Amiraults of orchestrating a public relations campaign, but the campaign didn't work, he informed reporters. "I am happy for the 13 brave young children who testified at two trials about the terrible things that happened to them at Fells Acres, " he told them. "What is important is that the children have been validated. Their testimony has been validated."

Fells Acres parents gave television interviews. "They can stay in jail till they all die, " one declared. "They can be executed." Her teenage son still lived through the experience he had at Fells Acres, another told a reporter.

From the moment the decision was published, it became clear that the liberally inclined Supreme Judicial Court of Massachusetts had set a precedent of sorts with this decision. All the astonishment and shock it produced centered on the same point: the proposition that whether justice was done in a case was less important than the necessity of bringing that case to a close.

From Violet's prison notes, November 1988:

Today my daughter Cheryl has started a retreat at this prison. She is with God from 8 A.M. till 9 P.M. each day.

She has more to offer than I do. I feel I am contaminated with my bitterness.

I woke up at 5:15. I go over this shattering of our lives—there is no relief. I think of nothing else. It is all pain.

Wenatchee

How the Wenatchee investigations began is not easy to unravel even today. What is clear is that the now-famous roundup of Wenatchee citizens, all to be charged as child molesters, had its beginning in 1995 in the single-minded efforts of Robert Perez, sex crimes investigator for the Wenatchee police, and the like-minded staff of the local Child Protective Services in this town nestled in the foothills of Washington's Cascade Mountains, population 59,000. Of those charged, most were poor and indigent. Few could afford an attorney, and all would see their children taken from them.

The investigation and prosecutions quickly won the full backing of community leaders, the entire legal establishment, and the impassioned support of the town's one newspaper, the Wenatchee World. That there was no way to know what the suspects said when they were first questioned or what their interrogator said was not a problem. It was his custom, Detective Perez explained, to destroy original notes of his interviews. Nor did he keep audiotapes. Perez instead offered summaries which he composed himself, based, he explained, on what the suspect told him. That too was the form of the confessions that he offered. Still, nothing done or undone in these investigations dampened official enthusiasm for the cases Perez built. Wenatchee police chief Ken Badgley expressed his full support. The town mayor, Earl Tilly, issued a declaration in which he noted that the child victims in Wenatchee had suffered losses no less terrible than those suffered in the Oklahoma City bombing. As to critics of the investigations, the mayor explained that there were people of questionable motive prone to engage in "police bashing." Judge Carol Wardell broke down weeping while sentencing one sex ring defendant. The judge explained later that she had been moved to tears by her anger at people skeptical about these cases.

Of the many official pronouncements, none was more intriguing than the one from the head of the Wenatchee Chamber of Commerce, Melanie Shaw, also apparently outraged that people outside the community had begun to raise questions about the charges. The leader of that organization

now insisted, with considerable fervor, that whatever anybody might say, Wenatchee certainly *was* home to a huge sex
ring peopled by degenerates operating all over town. It is not
easy to recall when the world last heard a chamber of commerce insistent on the truth of such a claim. Under the circumstances, those critical of the roundups and arrests were
destined to have no easy time of it. Still, some in Wenatchee
were willing. This small but intransigent bunch raised questions about the arrests, demanded accountability, and tried
to find defense lawyers worthy of the name, and for this they
would face no little hostility themselves. In a town inflamed
over daily newspaper accounts of predators molesting children—a community heartfelt in its gratitude to the authorities who had brought them to justice—raising questions
about the police, and even about the truth of these charges,
was a clear invitation to trouble.

Connie and Mario Fry, leaders of the group, managed to
live serenely enough, despite a car window shot out, a living
room window shattered by a thrown rock, eggs tossed at their
house, anonymous warning letters. During the regular meetings held at the Frys, a Mormon family, police cars slowly cir-
cled the house, while an officer recorded the license plates of
the cars in the driveway. The oldest Fry daughter begged her
parents to send her younger brothers and sisters to live with
her out of state before Child Protective Services could file an
accusation and have them taken away to foster care.

Her parents refused, though they knew the girl's fears were not unfounded. To run afoul of Perez and his allies at Child Protective Services was a proven danger. Any counselor or other child services caseworker expressing skepticism about the charges could expect trouble. At the very least, they were to be forbidden all contact with the children involved lest they undermine the prosecution of these cases. All this was in accordance with a 1994 order, issued by the state's Department of Social and Health Services, that children were to be removed immediately from counseling with any staff member harboring doubts about the allegations. One of the rare Child Protective Services workers to raise doubts about the validity of a charge soon found his career ended, himself among the accused. Otherwise, the child services agencies had no lack of counselors who could satisfy the requirement for absolute belief.

———

Whatever side they took, most people in Wenatchee agreed that the blond, rosy-cheeked Detective Perez could never have uncovered as many cases of molestation as he had without the aid of sisters Donna and Melinda Everett, ages eight and ten—the accusers and chief witnesses in most of the cases. That these young prosecution witnesses also happened to be Detective Perez's own foster daughters and members of his household appeared not to trouble anyone in Wenatchee's law enforcement establishment. In 1992, one girl had already given fanciful testimony in another case—testimony that nonetheless ended in a child rape conviction. In 1994, she came to live in the comfortable home of Detective Perez and his wife, where she was soon joined by her older sister.

In January 1995, the younger girl began confiding new names of molesters to an attentive Detective Perez, who had just been named chief sex abuse investigator. Perez and two child care workers subsequently took the girl on a ride around town, a journey reminiscent of the one taken in the McMartin case, where children had fingered half the population of Manhattan Beach, California. The girl was now asked to point out to Detective Perez all the locations in which she and other children had been assaulted. By the end of this journey, which came to be known to local skeptics as The Parade of Homes, the girl had identified twenty-three sites, the church and the home of local pastor Robert Roberson among them, as well as a molester or two she saw passing by on the sidewalk. All this information the child care workers carefully recorded.

In court, the girl held a large teddy bear while testifying against her half-sister, a terrified woman in her thirties. As the woman slowly shook her head, the young witness gave details of the woman's alleged sexual assaults. Troubled by a heavy cough, the child nevertheless appeared radiant. Her foster father, Detective Perez, smiled encouragingly from the prosecutors' table, and at the rear of the courtroom, Child Protective Services workers beamed, silently urging her on.

The prosecutors had, altogether, a core of four child witnesses giving testimony about the sex ring. Each child taking the stand came with a teddy bear, and each received waves and thumbs-up signs from Wenatchee's Child Protective Services personnel who helped develop the cases, avidly believed in the accusations, and packed the courtroom at every trial.

Within the first few months of investigation, more than forty people were arrested on similar charges—several charged with 2,400 and more counts of sex abuse. One woman was charged with 3,200 counts of child rape—a lifetime's work. Within months, Child Protective Services placed fifty children of the accused in foster care.

In this regard as others, no other agency provided more dedicated service to the prosecutors than Child Protective Services. With agency approval, some children of the accused were taken off to locked facilities (inaccessible to their parents' defense attorneys and family members) to undergo therapy. The benefits to the children would be hard to ascertain. The therapeutic advantages to the prosecutors were, on the other hand, clear enough: the children's treatment consisted mostly of efforts to induce them to give details of their parents' sexual crimes.

Of the accused, some plea-bargained and some confessed, faced with threats of a lifetime in prison and loss of their children. Many soon recanted those strangely stilted confessions studded with elaborate descriptions of child molestation orgies and the names of all the townspeople supposedly involved in those activities.

The list of suspected molesters grew apace.

———

Middle-aged Wenatchee resident Robert Devereaux became a suspect early in the investigations. A former businessman, he had given the most reluctant of consents when his wife decided they should run a group foster home. But by the time of their divorce, Devereaux had apparently found the work of his life. A social worker who had watched him at that work concluded that he was the rarest of foster parents—the kind who did not burn out. There were, the same source said, no fewer than 200 girls in Wenatchee who owed thanks to him, and him alone, for the only stability and support they had ever known in their lives.

Of the alleged crimes charged to Devereaux, his former

foster daughter Nikki scornfully declared, "This is a man who cared about discipline and modesty and about us. This is a man who went without all year and bought nothing for himself so he could give us—we were all girls—a proper Christmas."

Devereaux's problems began, in fact, precisely because the residents of his foster home were all girls, a fact that caught Perez's attention. Shortly after his divorce, the foster home they once praised as exemplary became, for Child Protective Services workers, an object of darkest suspicion. CPS workers went to schools attended by Devereaux's foster children to ask them if he had exposed himself to them and worse. In July 1994, Detective Perez arrested Devereaux and charged him with hundreds of counts of child rape and molestation, all connected with the sex ring circle alleged to hold its meetings at his house—among many others in town. By the time Devereaux faced trial, twenty-two people had already been sent to prison, a number for very long terms. Nine more awaited trial, and no one knew how many more were to follow them. It was clear to Devereaux, charged with numerous frightful crimes against children, that he faced long years in prison if convicted. Unwilling to take the risk and with the police eager for confessions, Devereaux agreed to confess to two counts, both extraordinary for their triviality. He agreed to plead guilty to the spanking of one child and the charge of "rendering criminal assistance" (he had warned someone he might be arrested). Why, the bitter Devereaux wondered, would a man the police had accused of the most brutal multiple sex assaults be allowed to walk away with this slap on the wrist if they thought there was any truth to the charges? It was a question that needed no answer, Devereaux knew, as he sat in his darkened house, sold to pay the lawyers, a house empty of furniture, sold off to pay the bills—a free man and also a ruined one like many another in Wenatchee.

For all their lack of official constraints, the sex ring investigators had their problems. The mere existence of a group like the one led by Mario and Connie Fry was trouble, not to mention their activities, which included spreading word about the interrogations and the dictated confessions. So, too, was their alliance with a reporter for KREM 2 News, a CBS affiliate, Tom Grant, a local TV reporter who would, alone of all local journalists, pick up on the truth about the Wenatchee sex ring story and hammer away at it relentlessly. The group's members busied themselves collecting funds for the defense of the accused, many of them people on welfare.

Mario and Connie Fry wiped the spittle from their car windows, tuned out the jeering and blasting horns of Wenatchee residents who drove by their house to yell that this or that defendant was guilty as charged. They mortgaged their house to pay defense expenses for one accused couple. All this activity did not endear Mario Fry, employed at Wenatchee's Public Utilities District, to the agency managers, one of whom suggested strongly that it would be best if the Frys ceased their efforts on behalf of the accused. Fry replied with the countersuggestion that anyone there who didn't like his activities should in fact try to fire him for exercising his rights as a citizen.

"You'll make me a rich man," he told the manager.

Fry was not again troubled at work.

———

The trouble that found Paul Glassen at work was enduring in ways he could not have imagined at the time, and he was a man who knew enough to imagine a great deal. He was the caseworker who had described Devereaux's admirable work and the one who reported that Devereaux's daughter had come to his office to recant the accusations she had made. She had been willing to offer up lies about her foster father, she explained, because she was furious at his effort to discipline her.

For reporting this, Glassen was handcuffed and taken off to be booked on charges of "witness tampering." He became, also, instant persona non grata at Child Protective Services, from whose premises he was escorted. Child Protective Services supervisor Tim Abbey then proceeded to fire Glassen, alleging that he had failed to report other abuse, but even this did not bring him to full appreciation of the trouble in which he had put himself. This Glassen began to grasp when his name began showing up on the list of molesters identified by Detective Perez's witnesses. Soon descriptions of the molesters began to include references to "a guy named Paul. Paul said he worked at Child Protective Services."

Unlike most of those charged, Glassen was educated, and he could see the possibilities. For one, Child Protective Services could move to take his child away. This was enough possibility for him. In no time, he and his wife and five-year-old son were in a car headed for British Columbia, where his wife's family lived. At the time, he thought in a year he could well look back and see he'd been foolish to uproot his family, that his trouble with the agency would soon have blown over.

He was mistaken on all counts. The first months in British Columbia were pure misery—life in a basement apartment, with no money coming in. It didn't help to see the suspiciousness his wife's relatives exhibited toward him once they learned why the couple had abandoned Washington State. The main trouble had to do with work, which

Glassen found impossible to get for nearly a year and a half. Nor could he understand why, until he discovered the long reach of the Wenatchee investigators. Each time a prospective employer conducted a criminal behavior check, as social service agencies were all required to do, his name appeared along with a report. The employer could read in that report that Paul Glassen had been a suspect in the molestation of more than fifty children and that one of the children he was suspected of victimizing was his own. Employers who wanted more information were advised to get in touch with Detective Perez or with an investigator for Washington State's Department of Social and Health Service.

———

One of the first members of the Pentecostal Church of God House of Prayer to be charged was Sunday school teacher Honna Sims, accused of raping and molesting children during the group sex adventures alleged to have taken place at Pastor Robert Roberson's church every Friday and Sunday night. Each young accuser offered versions of these festivities, dazzling in their variety. One child claimed he was so tired from having to engage in sexual acts with all the adults at the church on weekends that the pastor would write a note to school to get him excused on Mondays. Another told of inflatable sex toys kept under the altar, of the pastor lying on stage crying "Hallelujah!" while attacking young victims during services, of mass child rape (at the church and elsewhere) by men all in black wearing sunglasses and by ladies wielding colored pencils and carrots, and of crowds of adults so organized that everybody got a turn with each of the children. Anyone who missed his turn with a child would get an extra visit that month.

Neither the fifty-year-old Roberson nor his forty-five-year-old wife, Connie, were altogether surprised when the police arrived to take them to the jail. Roberson had begun questioning the sex ring investigation when Perez obtained a long, articulate statement of confession from one of the pastor's parishioners—a woman, Roberson knew, of limited intelligence who could barely put two sentences together. The pastor's difficulties multiplied when it became clear that he was monitoring the investigations closely and keeping a record. His indefatigable record keeping on every arrest, every detail of every charge, on the history of the accusers, inevitably branded Roberson a troublemaker, to be added to the lengthening list of sex ring suspects.

In March 1995, the pastor stood up at a public meeting and loudly denounced the arrests and the investigators' tactics. Five days later, police took the Robersons to jail, where they were kept on a million dollars bail each and where

Robert Roberson was regularly beaten up, the guards having informed prisoners of the child molester in their midst.

The Robersons were imprisoned on charges that they had committed sexual assaults on their own four-and-a-half-year-old daughter and an eleven-year-old girl—charges that would in due course multiply to include sex crimes of a staggering variety. The number of their alleged victims would multiply, too, as the Robersons' young accusers told rapt police and CPS investigators of more and more children abused in corners and crevices of the pastor's small church; of child rape in more conspicuous places, including the altar, during services; and of orgies in a variety of other locations around town.

Following their arrest, the Robersons' daughter, Rebekah, was taken off to a foster home and given over to the ministrations of Child Protective Services and allied abuse investigators. The latter's interrogations soon enough produced the results they sought. The investigators could report that Rebekah had made a disclosure of sexual assaults committed by her parents.

———

Pastor Robert Roberson and Connie Roberson went on trial in November 1995. The prosecutors charged that the couple hosted parties of adults who gathered weekly to assault as many as fifty children at their church. These revelries took place, it was alleged, following services Friday through Sunday nights, at which time Pastor Roberson would order everyone into the basement to undress. So directed, scores of adults would line up to commit sexual acts with children, after which, the accusers reported, hot cocoa and cookies were served.

The trial was a pivotal one for the prosecutors, involving as it did the most sensational of all the alleged sex crimes unearthed by Wenatchee's chief sex abuse investigator, Perez— mass assaults on children. It was therefore no trifling matter when the state discovered that they would be deprived of the two chief witnesses against the pastor and his wife. First came news that the child whose accusations were the basis of nearly all the sex ring cases—Detective Perez's own eleven-year-old foster daughter—had had a breakdown and had to be placed in a psychiatric hospital. She would not again be giving court testimony, a spokesman declared. This left the other child witness against the Robersons, and this one had a credibility problem too dangerous for the state to ignore. A regular witness for the prosecution in the sex ring cases, she had recently admitted under cross-examination that she had made false rape charges against both her foster father and her psychological counselor. That counselor himself then testified that the girl had threatened to tell people he had molested other children.

The prosecutors moved quickly to solve their witness problem. Days before the scheduled start of the trial, they announced that the case against the Robersons had been amended to include four new victims. Seventeen additional counts of child rape and molestation were now charged to the defendants. The list of the new victims to testify included the Robersons' five-year-old daughter, Rebekah.

The last time the defendants had any contact with their child was the day they were arrested. Roberson was cuffed outside his church while distributing supplies from the food bank he ran for the poor. Rebekah was taken into custody by Child Protective Services and interrogated by a therapist. By the fourth session, the therapist reported that she was able to determine that the child had been sexually molested. Whatever the girl actually said in the interview, and how she came to say it, only the therapist knew. She had made no recording of the interviews.

The new list of witnesses against the Robersons included an adult who would give detailed descriptions of the action at the church. Gary Filbeck, a repeat sex offender who not long before had been arrested for first-degree rape, had struck a highly advantageous deal (charges reduced to assault and a sentence of under one year) in exchange for testimony in this and other sex ring cases. Filbeck would provide some of the most colorful accusations in this case—no small distinction. According to this witness, Pastor Roberson had stripped and raped children onstage during services, while declaiming, "This will drive the devil out!" Filbeck also provided numerous and rich descriptions of the pastor's sexual climaxes and the accompanying cries of exultation from the congregation.

He was now the only adult witness—and the key witness—against the Robersons. The prosecutors declared in their amended charges that in his statement, "Mr. Filbeck describes being present at the Pentecostal Church and observing Robert Roberson sexually molest R.R." (his daughter, Rebekah). Further, they had Filbeck's testimony that "Connie Roberson was present, and by her presence and words encouraged and assisted the acts of Robert Roberson." Mrs. Roberson herself stood accused of fifteen acts of rape and molestation.

The jurors heard the prosecutors' description of the sexual abuse the Robersons had inflicted on their own child and how it had all been uncovered. Following her parents' arrest, the child was given sex education therapy. During this treatment, administered when the child was in state custody, counselor Donna Anderson introduced the child, then four and a half years old, to a picture book with graphic illustrations of men and women cohabiting and with details about hardening penises and the like. Ms. Anderson had been moved to introduce this book, she explained, out of her belief that the child had been molested by her father.

Overall, the state prosecutors did not conceal their view that the social class to which the pastor and the congregants of this church belonged bore a direct relation to their crimes. In his closing argument, the Douglas County prosecutor said that the stains on the church carpet could have been vaginal discharge or possibly urine. Perhaps, the prosecutor said, the people who attended this church were given to urinating on the floor. It was not the first time such comments had been voiced about this church and its congregation, most of them welfare clients, without education, and in other ways at the lowest rungs of the social ladder.

While holding forth on his investigations of the Pentecostal Church of God House of Prayer prior to the trial, Douglas County sheriff Dan LaRoche told one reporter, "Yes, it's a church. But the congregation is broke. The church is a mess, a real dump. It's not like we busted Notre Dame." Early in the trial, prosecutors introduced some fifty slides showing the unkempt grounds of the church—presumably in the hope of shoring up their contentions about the manifold evils taking place inside. The Robersons' defense attorney, Robert Van Siclen, argued—in vain—that the slides could conceivably be relevant, but only if the defendants had been charged with littering.

For all their advantages—among them a judge clearly hostile to the defense—the prosecutors had their problems, including a number of prosecution witnesses who seemed to end up, in effect, as witnesses for the defense, leaving trial observers wondering what had impelled the prosecutors to call them. These included members of the Washington State Patrol and other experts who came to testify at great length about forensic light sources, laser equipment, and other advanced methods employed in their effort to find traces of semen in the church. When their exhaustive testimony finally ended, these prosecution experts offered their conclusions: no trace of semen was to be found in the church.

A thirteen-year-old witness for the state took the stand to testify that she had seen nothing untoward at the church, which she had stopped attending only because she was worried about enough time to do her homework. But, the prosecutor asked, hadn't she told investigators from his office that she remembered feeling uncomfortable at the church? No, she had not, the witness replied. Another prosecution witness maintained that he had been sexually assaulted by Pastor Roberson, a claim seriously undermined by the revelation that he had been confined in an institution 150 miles away at the time of the supposed molestation. When asked to identify the pastor who had raped him, the witness pointed to defense attorney Robert Van Siclen. In the end, the prosecutors affirmed their full confidence in Gary Filbeck, the convicted child molester who got a deal in exchange for his testimony. He was, they declared, their key witness. "It takes a sex offender to catch a sex offender," explained one state attorney.

———

Jurors took somewhere between four and five hours to acquit Pastor Robert Roberson and Connie Roberson of all fourteen charges of child rape and molestation brought against them, though they had in fact required nothing like this much time to come to their verdict. "It was," a juror dryly reported, "not a difficult decision for us."

The case went to the jury at 7:30 P.M. on a Friday, after which time a foreman was chosen, a pizza consumed, a straw poll taken. Monday morning, all twelve voted for full acquittal on the first poll. They would make no secret of their reasons. Neither prosecutors nor police, they charged, had troubled to investigate the merits of the accusations made against the Robersons. "There was nothing to this case," a juror observed. "Why did they bring this trial? Here were all these people who had attended every church service for the past three or four years, who had never seen anything like what the prosecution was describing, and the prosecutors had never even talked to any of them."

The defense prevailed despite the extraordinary restrictions placed on its attorneys by Judge T. W. "Chip" Small, who refused to allow any discussion of tainting of witnesses or references to interviewers who led children. The Robersons were now permitted to claim their child, whom they had been forbidden to contact in the nine months since their arrest—though they would still have to allow investigators to inspect and make home visits.

Most other Wenatchee defendants who went to trial would not see so successful an outcome. The Robersons were represented pro bono by Robert Van Siclen, a singularly talented Seattle attorney appalled by the case—precisely the kind who could make jurors wonder why it had ever been brought, who could, in his soft-spoken way, bring home to them the absurdity of a prosecution in which the state never bothered talking to the parishioners. Attorneys of this kind were unavailable to most other Wenatchee defendants, who had to make do with state-appointed lawyers who were undertrained and, with an exception or two, uninterested in serious combat with state prosecutors. The few defendants able to hire experienced attorneys, usually gifts of local philanthropists, were the fortunate ones. Indeed, no one charged who had a private attorney ended up going to prison. One of the several frightened accused who had signed confessions under interrogation by Detective Perez was twenty-eight-year-old Susan Everett. A Wenatchee citizen infuriated by this prosecution retained one of Seattle's more prominent attorneys to represent her. With John Henry Brown on the scene dealing with the Wenatchee prosecutors, Everett soon had little to worry about compared to what might have been her fate otherwise. She was charged with a misdemeanor and sentenced to less than a year.

Ralph Gausvik, whose house was among those Detective Perez's foster daughter pointed to during her drive around town, was found guilty on all counts. This outcome did not surprise anyone who had seen the performance of his state-appointed defense counsel. Remarkably enough, though Gausvik's trial was held at the height of the furor over Detective Perez's interrogations, the defense attorney managed a cross-examination of Perez without asking a single question. If the accused's defense attorney had no questions about Detective Perez's tactics, why should the jury have any? Gausvik, who maintained his innocence and who signed no confession, was sentenced to twenty years.

Mark and Carol Doggett were not considered part of the sex ring circle. Their trouble with Detective Perez and the law began when the couple decided they should seek help from Child Protective Services upon discovering that their difficult thirteen-year-old son had forced himself on his younger sister. In short order, Child Protective Services concluded that the son was not the problem; rather, the parents had been molesting all their children. The youngest of their five children was the first to be taken off to be interrogated. In due course, the Doggetts stood charged with raping their children nightly. The oldest of the children, seventeen-year-old Sarah "Sam" Doggett, became an object of hot pursuit by Child Protective Services personnel since she appeared on local television to denounce the charges against her mother and father as ludicrous. The day after her television appearance, Child Protective Services personnel came looking for her. The eldest Doggett daughter hid out at the apartment of a relative, far from Wenatchee. There she raged at the "memory recovery" treatment given her small sisters to help them remember details of abuse. Sam had herself been carted off to a locked facility, in order, the therapists explained, to help her to overcome her denial of her parents' sexual abuse.

That her parents were devout Mormons did not help their case. At home in the mornings, the Doggett girl recalled, the family took part in a prayer circle in which each child asked God's help for the challenge of the day ahead. It was not a memory that would have impressed the Child Protective Services personnel. Indeed, it was the view of a considerable quarter of the child care establishment and Child Protective Services personnel in Wenatchee that Mormons were to be viewed with suspicion—as a cult given to sexual abuse and, at the very least, to other degrading and un-healthful influences on children.

Child Protective Services supervisor Tim Abbey was present, along with Detective Perez, when Mark Doggett was picked up and interrogated. It was soon clear to Perez that Doggett would not confess and would continue to maintain his innocence. Perez then proceeded to inform him in vivid detail the nature of the sexual attacks he could suffer in prison if he didn't confess to his crimes. Doggett first had the idea, when he saw Tim Abbey, chief supervisor of We-natchee's Child Protective Services, that this official was there as a mediator—someone he would be able to appeal to. He was, after all, a social worker. How mistaken he was be-came clear soon enough as Abbey himself began describing the treatment Doggett could expect in prison if he didn't confess now.

Detectives, he understoond, made such threats—but a social work administrator? When the interrogation finally ended, Abbey announced that he was now going home to his wife and family and that Detective Perez was going home to his, but as a result of his refusal to admit guilt, Doggett would be going to prison.

The Child Protective Services official had no doubt that the Doggett children were raped nightly by their parents. Ac-cording to the charges elicited from the youngest Doggett child, then age eight, Mark and Carol Doggett made their children line up outside their bedroom every night so they could take turns coming in to engage in sexual acts with their parents.

In 1995, Mark and Carol Doggett were found guilty, each given a sentence of ten years and ten months. They were sentenced by Carol Wardell, the judge who had been moved to tears of rage that there could be people who failed to believe the truth of the sex ring charges.

———

In time, the appeals courts overturned one conviction after another. In 1997, the young New York appellate attorney Robert Rosenthal, by now one of the leading experts in these cases, won a reversal of Carol Doggett's conviction. Attorney Eric Nielsen won a reversal of Mark Doggett's conviction.

The Washington State papers, which had paid little or no attention to the Wenatchee cases at the height of the investigations and roundups, in time began to turn out comprehensive investigative pieces on the story. There were calls for state investigations. In 1998, a state appeals court appointed Whitman County Superior Court judge Wallis Friel to hold hearings into the conduct of the investigations and the evidence against one couple, which became a commentary on all the cases. Harold and Idella Everett were central figures in this story, not least because they were the parents of the girls who had made all the accusations. In his findings, a lethal description of the behavior of Child Protective Services therapists, counselors, and state witnesses, the judge enumerated in elaborate detail the accusations of the state's two star witnesses, Donna and her sister, Melinda, and concluded that "no rational trier of fact would believe these allegations."

Ralph Gausvik, who had wept throughout his trial, been sentenced to twenty years, and refused all offers of a guilty plea, won release when Rosenthal filed a petition in his behalf.

After his exoneration, Pastor Robert Roberson embarked on an unyielding legal battle on behalf of those still imprisoned. With his copious records, his unequaled grasp of the details and overall history of this affair, Roberson proved an indispensable guide for attorneys working on the criminal and civil cases.

Caseworker Paul Glassen, who had fled Wenatchee with his wife and child, ultimately found a job, notwithstanding the computer listing him as a suspected abuser. Late in the summer of 1996, when he had gone jobless for a year, he approached the adminstrator of the Canadian social agency who had just hired him and with trepidation informed her of what she would be finding in the criminal background check. That check would mention a felony, the charge of police obstruction, and the fact that he was suspected of molesting fifty children. She listened to this recital without interruption, and when it was over, she had but one question for Glassen: Did this mean he would now be able to start full time?

Glassen remains employed at the agency, grateful, still, for the memory of that moment. He received a settlement of a few hundred thousand dollars from the city of Wenatchee and a letter declaring that he was not involved in or suspected of crimes of child sex abuse.

Former businessman and foster father Robert Devereaux, who took the minor plea and sold his house to pay his lawyer, lived an impoverished man thereafter. He was invited to live in a small apartment belonging to one of his grateful foster daughters, now married, and found employment at a service station, where he still works.

Cited in numerous civil suits still pending against the city of Wenatchee, Detective Robert Perez retired on disability.

Perez's star witnesses, Donna and Melinda Everett, returned to live with their biological parents, Harold and Idella Everett. Now in their late teens, the former witnesses have publicly declared that none of the crimes they described ever took place.

The Amiraults, Part Three

A month after the decision, the Amirault women's new attorneys filed a petition for rehearing, which the Supreme Judicial Court not unexpectedly rejected. Violet and Cheryl began spending their days getting rid of such possessions of normal life as they had acquired in the twenty months since they had emerged from prison. They packed, stored, sold, gave away, and otherwise prepared for their imminent rearrest and return to Framingham. They busied themselves thus because they were inveterate planners, laser-like in their focus on every likely possibility and need—Violet's training made manifest—and they did so to dull their certain knowledge that the state police could be at the door at any moment. When they would be taken into custody, they had no idea.

Nor had they any idea of the struggle just beginning between defiant Superior Court justices (the trial judges) who had determined that the Amiraults had been convicted on baseless charges and the Supreme Judicial Court. The first phase began when the Court overturned Barton's order vacating the women's conviction. The Supreme Judicial Court next refused to review its decision reinstating the conviction. Having no other recourse, attorney James Sultan filed another motion for a new trial.

Violet and Cheryl were not now overwhelmed by terror at the thought of going to prison as when they were sent away ten years earlier; they now knew what they could expect. There was another way in which things had changed. Violet was a first-generation American, the child of immigrants from Sette de Roma who had grown up imbued with ideas about democracy and citizenship. Every child who attended her school was required to begin the day reciting the Pledge of Allegiance. Her idea of what it meant to be an American citizen remained with her even when she was most powerless, an outcast from society, a prisoner of the state. Her fury at the state was bottomless. They had sent its agents barging into her school on the basis of a phoned accusation. They had confiscated her records, arrested her son without questioning, closed the school down before she and her family even went on trial, and finally made her a prisoner—and for all that, she had lost none of her very American expectation that justice would triumph.

In the summer of 1987 when she and Cheryl were first shackled and taken off to Framingham, Violet had an idea that at the last, it would not be allowed, that her fellow citizens would be moved to do something. Later, she thought that she could actually remember people running after the car, shouting, "Where are you taking those women?" Now, she entertained no such ideas. The marshals would come and take her and Cheryl, she knew, and there would be no one and nothing to stop it.

The grounds for the new trial motion this time concerned the former attorneys' failure to raise the confrontation issue and the children's seating, at either trial or on first appeal. The grounds for the motion rested, in short, on ineffective assistance of counsel, generally considered the plea of last resort and one difficult to win.

On May 5, 1997, the new motion came, as was appropriate, before the judge who had been appointed to replace the Amirault women's retired trial judge. It came, that is, to Justice Robert A. Barton, who had thrown out the women's conviction twenty months earlier. A man who knew his way around the system, he spent little time pondering the new decision. He knew what he had to do and what should happen next, with any luck.

Violet and Cheryl came to the courtroom dressed for prison, in regulation black and white. If the decision went against them, they were to be taken into custody immediately.

Justice Barton addressed the packed courtroom in steely tones. After a discussion of the motions before him, he got to the first point. The Supreme Judicial Court had vacated his order granting the women a new trial. He then delivered his view: "These women did not receive a fair trial and justice was not done." A trial procedure must conform to constitutional requirements whether the trial involved "a death penalty or a day in jail," he declared.

More than a few people listening recognized the death penalty reference as a thrust aimed directly at the Supreme Judicial Court justices and their now-famous last decision—a reminder of the possible consequences of a court's devotion to the principle of finality.

His views on this case stated, Justice Barton announced that he would now recuse himself from the case and have no further involvement. He was moved to make this decision, he explained, because he had to wonder whether his impartiality might now be questioned. He had concluded he could not consider himself impartial in considering the motions before the court this day.

In fact, the reason for his decision to recuse himself was

more complicated. Barton worried that if he granted a second new trial motion, it would be perceived as the act of a biased judge. It would not help the Amiraults and would be all the more quickly overturned. What was required now was a new trial order from some *other* Superior Court judge, and there was a good chance, under the circumstances, that the Amiraults and their attorney would encounter one. It happened, as Justice Barton had figured out, that the justice in line to decide the motion in the event a new judge was required would be Isaac Borenstein, another close student of the case.

Violet and Cheryl and their surprised attorneys departed from Justice Barton's courtroom along with a throng of reporters and television crews and headed, as directed, to another courtroom two floors down. There they found themselves in front of Justice Borenstein, assigned to hear their motion for a new trial.

In rejecting the claim that the Amiraults had been denied the right to face their accusers, the Supreme Judicial Court had argued that their original attorneys had failed to make this objection at the trial and suggested they might have deliberately chosen to do this for strategic reasons.

The Amiraults' attorneys came to court armed with testimony not often given to appellate lawyers arguing ineffective assistance of counsel. They had the affidavits of the two trial lawyers who had represented Violet and Cheryl, Joseph J. Balliro and Juliane Balliro; both, remarkably enough, were prepared to attest that they had in fact committed a serious error in the representation of their clients. Further, they averred, their failure to protect their clients was no part of any tactical decision.

None of this was much reassurance for the attorneys or their clients. Justice Barton's recusal had been shocking to them. He had become a symbol of hope. They had no idea what they could expect from the new judge. The defeat at the hands of the Supreme Judicial Court was fresh and weighed on their spirits, as did the state police car waiting outside in preparation for Violet and Cheryl's return to Framingham. James Sultan and his clients entered the new judge's courtroom hoping that Justice Borenstein would at least allow the women to remain free on bail while he considered their motion for a new trial. This he did.

Four days later, Borenstein granted a new trial, overturning the women's conviction. In the courtroom, instant media bedlam ensued. As in Newburyport, Violet and her daughter were besieged by well-wishers, hailed by passing truckers who heard the news bulletin, cheered by motorists hanging out of cars with their thumbs up. Next to the Amiraults, their lawyers, the McGonagles, and their friends, who were all ecstatic, no one was more pleased with the way the day turned out than Justice Robert Barton.

Violet and Cheryl returned to the homes they had thought, earlier that morning, they would not see again for years. As they expected, Justice Borenstein's decision brought immediate word from District Attorney Tom Reilly that the Commonwealth of Massachusetts would appeal. "The families and the children feel," he told reporters, "as if another stake has been driven through their hearts."

When a decision came in the women's case, the inevitable question that arose was what it might mean for Gerald. That his prospects of freedom were far more remote than those of his mother and sister had long been clear to his lawyers and everyone else who knew the case. When people still thought Violet and Cheryl would be going back to prison, before Judge Borenstein issued the new trial ruling, there was speculation in the Boston press and elsewhere that the women would perhaps soon be granted parole and that this would be a deal the prosecutors could live with. Violet, now nearly seventy-five years old, and her daughter could go free, and Gerald, who had received the heaviest sentence by far, as males in these cases invariably did, would remain in prison.

On a Sunday television talk show about the Amirault case, a panelist described his gut feeling that the women were innocent and Gerald guilty. How he had come to his gut feeling—all three members of the family, after all, had been charged with the same horrific sexual crimes—the panelist did not say. Nor was it necessary to say; anyone listening would instinctively have grasped that the reason for the gut feeling was that Gerald was a man. Feelings like this were not uncommon among people who believed that dark crimes must have been committed at Fells Acres, just as the prosecutors said, but who had trouble dealing with the picture of the elderly Violet raping a four year old anally with a sharp stick while the whole school watched—a crime of which she was convicted—or of Cheryl Amirault committing similar brutal crimes.

All such concerns about Violet Amirault were soon rendered irrelevant. On May 9, Violet and Cheryl walked out of court free for the moment. The prosecutors filed the inevitable appeal, Cheryl tried to find a job, and Violet settled down to deal with her financial situation, which was dire. She took comfort in the hope that she might be able to get at the social security payments withheld during the eight years of imprisonment, but it would take time, the attorneys advised her.

Time, it turned out, was what she did not have. Months earlier, Violet had begun to suffer serious loss of appetite and severe nausea, all symptoms, people assured her, caused by stress, entirely natural under the circumstances. She lived, to be sure, in a state of perpetual anxiety now—not only or even primarily about money as much as what would happen when the Supreme Judicial Court acted on the prosecutors' appeal. Violet believed, though she kept it from her children, that in the end, the police would be at the door to take them back to Framingham. Why would the Supreme Judicial Court not strike down Justice Borenstein's ruling and again order the convictions reinstated?

When Violet's symptoms became acute in early summer, a medical examination revealed inoperable abdominal cancer. On September 12, she lay on a couch, tended by Cheryl, in a room crowded with photographs of better days—pictures of the sun-worshipping Violet, laughing, on a boat, in a park, surrounded by her large Italian family, pictures of Violet with Gerald and Cheryl, and a number of photographs of Fells Acres. Waxen and drugged, she heaved her body up from the couch once or twice and then fell back. By the morning, she was gone. Gerald, permitted to leave prison for the first time since his entry, was taken to the funeral home in leg chains so that he could say goodbye to his mother.

One month later, the Amiraults' attorneys filed another motion for a new trial for Cheryl, this one based on the ground that discoveries had come to light that had not been available when the Amiraults were tried. The attorneys in effect argued that they now had new evidence to present on the subject of children's testimony, and the results of scholarship and experiments, relevant to this issue.

The prosecutors, too, filed a motion before the Supreme Judicial Court, this one asking that Cheryl be returned to prison immediately. The court decided to defer decision on the prosecutors' motion. The justices decided that a special hearing should be held on the merits of the new evidence, with Isaac Borenstein to preside.

The Supreme Judicial Court's action, which effectively kept the Amiraults' appeal open, was made, many in Massachusetts's legal community guessed, in reaction to the uproar over the "finality" decision. Whatever the cause, Cheryl's attorneys had now been given the opportunity to present a case-by-case examination of each child witness's background and testimony. The arguments now did not concern constitutional issues of confrontation or ineffective assistance of counsel—matters that passed muster as grounds for appeal because they were new—but they were not the core issues on which the case turned. The entire case against the Amiraults was built on the children's testimony. To be able to show how that testimony was obtained was to get to the heart of the matter. Enthusiastic, the appellate attorneys made extensive plans for the hearing and spent long hours analyzing witnesses and exhibits.

The prosecutors were less keen. Confronted with this turn of events, District Attorney Tom Reilly made an unusual application to the Middlesex clerk of courts: he asked that a judge other than Isaac Borenstein be assigned to the hearing, a request the clerk denied.

In February 1998, Cheryl's attorneys presented expert witnesses, led by memory specialist Maggie Bruck, along with exhibits of the children's interviews. The commonwealth declined the opportunity to present its own expert witnesses. Outside the courtroom where attorney Dan Williams showed videotapes of the children's interrogations, an overflow knot of reporters gathered to watch the proceedings on television.

As they listened to the investigator's insistent pleas to tell the bad things and the resulting stories about slaughtered animals and stabbings and magic pills, a journalist howled, "Oh, my God!" "Did you hear that?" they asked one another in disbelief.

People who knew anything about the case required no experts or reference to new scholarship to bring home what was already entirely obvious about the testimony against the Amiraults. For those who did not, the hearings provided an education. Its more significant result by far was the thick report Justice Borenstein issued three months later, along with his rulings, a rigorously detailed document focusing on the experience of each child witness from the first interrogations on to the trial. Justice Borenstein did not trouble to conceal his views of the prosecutors' case: "The Amirault family was targeted in this investigation from the outset in a climate of fear and panic chronicled in pervasive and substantial media . . . coverage. Law enforcement officials had decided from the start that the Amiraults had committed these crimes."

As to the questioning of the children, who had been bombarded with pleas to tell about abuse, the justice wrote, "All of the child witnesses initially—and quite amazingly—withstood the barrage: they all denied any abuse. Eventually—and now we understand predictably—they were broken down." His comments on one child's experience summed up his views of the way all had been questioned: "Every trick in the book was used to get the child to say what the investigators—and eventually her parents—wanted her to say, rather than to learn, in a fair manner whether anything had actually happened to her."

Cheryl Amirault LeFave was entitled to a new trial, Justice Borenstein ruled. Furthermore, he said, none of the testimony of the child witnesses, now declared "forever tainted," would be allowable in any future trial. Also included in his decision this day was a declaration exonerating the deceased Violet Amirault of all charges.

The judge's decision precluding future use of the children's testimony would make another trial impossible in the unlikely event the prosecutors were prepared to hold one. Justice Borenstein's findings and the ruling freeing Cheryl were front-page news in Boston. District Attorney Tom Reilly announced he would be filing an immediate appeal.

On May 6, 1999, members of the Supreme Judicial Court heard oral arguments on the prosecutors' appeal. After Assistant DA Lynn Rooney's presentation, which boiled down to the contention that the children had not been led into accusations of abuse, attorney Daniel Williams rose to make his. The gentle manner in which Rooney had been questioned fell away. Justice Charles Fried had a question for attorney Williams, its tone heavy with exasperation. It was the business of justices to pose provocative questions during oral arguments, but as his questioning continued, it grew clear that something other than a wish to provoke intellectual exchange animated Fried. The Amiraults' attorney mentioned in passing what the parents of the accusing children felt. Justice Fried interrupted with a sneer. So now, he snapped, it was the *parents* who were the problem.

A spectator muttered, "The chickens have come home to roost," by which he meant the heat over the "finality" decision and Fried's resulting anger. The opinion had brought severe, not infreqently scathing, public censure. John Paul Sullivan, who had tried to free Violet and Cheryl, joined the fray to scoff at the decision and to say that both the women's and Gerald's convictions should have been thrown out. Three lower court justices—Barton, Borenstein, and the now retired John Paul Sullivan—had pitted themselves against the Supreme Judicial Court in this case.

Why, Justice Fried asked, should the Amirault attorney refer to this as an extraordinary case? Cases like this came before the court regularly, he maintained—cases "of parents, caretakers and boyfriends engaging in exactly the same kind of conduct that is charged here." And they came, he emphasized, "all the time."

In various quarters of the courtroom, people exchanged glances. Justice Fried had just declared that courts regularly heard charges that small children had been assaulted en masse in magic rooms by a family of molesters headed by an elderly nursery school head—children seduced and violated by assailants dressed as elephants, and photographed by clowns with big cameras and clowns who drank urine and ate feces. These, he suggested, were nothing more than the standard sorts of offenses charged to parents, caretakers, and boyfriends all the time. It was a patently ludicrous assertion, and one the justice himself could scarcely have believed— though acts of sexual abuse (none of them anything like the children's fantasies)—were nowadays charged to all sorts of people in all stations of life, doctors among them.

From Violet's notes, April 1989:

The catastrophe goes on. I have I feel outlived my usefulness on earth. I do not feel I can be of any help to my family. We have been caught up in the prison system which perpetuates itself as any business does. . . . I am eaten away with rage and hatred. I do not have enough space or time to vent it all. I am a demon of the worst kind. I have no space for anything or interest in this world. I actually want it to self destruct. I cannot utter any word without this poison coming through.

From Violet's notes, May 1989:

Today is Tooky's birthday. 35 years old. I remember everything so clearly re that day. The pregnancy—the recovery from surgery. . . . I think of all the joys my children brought me.

I spoke to Tooky on March 2. I really do not know how to talk to him. He is so positive. And I am bitter, enraged. . . . He is utterly destroyed and he tries to hide it from me. . . . How my heart breaks for my children.

From Violet's notes, May 1992:

Cheryl went to Parole Hearing. She overwhelmed them with her responses. "You are a very articulate and bright young lady," they told her.

But they denied her because she would not say she was guilty of a crime she never committed.

Patrick Griffin

Most people who knew Dr. Patrick Griffin would have guessed he had never heard of Linda Fairstein, renowned head of the Manhattan DA's Sex Crimes Unit or, for that matter, her agency. He had lived in New York for decades, one of those migrants to the city who seemed, forever, newcomers. There was a touch of reserve about him and also a hint of deference. It was one of the things about him his patients liked, as they did, even more, the degree of attention he paid them.

Those patients were shocked when, late on a Friday night in July 1995, Patrick Griffin was arrested, handcuffed, and taken off to a holding cell, charged with sexual assault of a patient. The forty-one-year-old internist was held in the old detention center known as the Tombs for some thirty hours, time enough for him to absorb the depths of the peril confronting him as a result of allegations made months before by a patient. He stood charged with the crime of oral sodomy, committed on a forty-three-year-old woman while performing a colonoscopy on her in his Central Park West office.

His arrest brought a flood of calls from patients who expressed incredulity or wanted to know what was going on. What the rest were thinking—the ones who didn't call—he would never know. The one thing clear was that everyone in his practice knew instantly that their internist had been arrested and was about to be charged as a sexual predator.

Few other crimes (except, perhaps, those of members of the clergy) are more certain to find a spot on the nightly news than those charged to doctors, especially if those crimes are sexual. This instance was no exception. Immediately after his arrest, the Manhattan District Attorney's Sex Crimes Unit provided a toll-free number, along with a message broadcast on radio and published in the New York Post, urging everyone who had a report to make about Dr. Griffin to come forward.

Released on bail, Patrick Griffin came home to a life utterly transformed. All through the summer and fall, one health maintenance organization after another sent letters announcing they had dropped him and would refuse to honor his bills. He was now without funds and without a practice. To earn money to pay the rent, he tended bar part-time and got work driving a truck on long hauls, a job that calmed his nerves somewhat. Having to scrounge ways to survive financially was a saving distraction—one that kept him from dwelling all day and all night on how his life had come to this.

This was not the sort of future anyone could have envisioned for the Oklahoma-born-and-bred Patrick Griffin, son of an oil pipeline worker of modest means. Educated in Tulsa Catholic schools like his numerous sisters and brothers, he proved an early achiever. By the age of sixteen, he was on his way out of Oklahoma bound for Columbia University, where he had a four-year scholarship. Following his graduation from Columbia Medical School, a residency at Columbia Presbyterian Hospital, and a fellowship at Harvard Medical School, he was appointed, at the age of thirty-three, director of fellowship training and internal medicine at St. Luke's–Roosevelt Hospital.

The question later asked—why he had not seen to it that a nurse was present during the colonoscopy—was no question to him. A board-certified internist, he generally had a nurse present when conducting vaginal or breast examinations. It had not occurred to him to view the colon as a sex organ.

His private office was necessarily modest, one of his employees told the court at his trial. This had a lot to do, she explained, with the doctor's habit of treating his patients whether they ever paid him or not—a tendency that caused the devoted office manager to sigh that he was not the best businessman.

Nor had he been the best equipped of men to deal with the trouble that would follow from the accusation against him. The conspicuously soft-spoken doctor proved no match for the deftness and sheer force of will of the patient he had treated since 1991—the patient who would end up, four and a half years later, filing a $10 million lawsuit against him.

It was not the first lawsuit filed by Christine Jeffreys, a forty-three-year-old woman with a checkered financial history. Temporarily evicted from her apartment in 1991 for nonpayment of rent, she claimed that this trauma had caused her to suffer stomach problems and assorted other forms of emotional anguish. On the basis of these claims, she filed a $2 million lawsuit against the apartment corporation. Soon after, she began seeing Dr. Griffin for stomach complaints and emotional stress, visits of no small importance for her civil suit against the landlord. As papers filed in that suit showed, Mrs. Jeffreys fully expected Dr. Griffin to testify to the physical and psychological damage she had suffered as a result of her eviction.

In this she was mistaken. Subpoenaed to provide such testimony in November 1994, Dr. Griffin informed her attorney that he could not subscribe to the claim that the eviction had caused Mrs. Jeffreys's pain and other complaints. It was the doctor's view that she suffered from depression, for which he prescribed Zoloft, an antidepressant.

A few weeks after the doctor's refusal to support her civil suit, she visited him again to say she was having stomach pains, whereupon she was given an appointment for a colonoscopy and an upper endoscopy. On the scheduled date, January 13, 1995, she arrived at Dr. Griffin's office suffering bouts of diarrhea and explained that she had had great difficulty consuming the prescribed colon cleanser, Golytely, a lot of which she had thrown up. This was not an uncommon problem among patients, the doctor would later testify.

Informed that she would arrive late, Dr. Griffin sped off to Roosevelt Hospital to perform another colonoscopy. He then returned to his office, administered the standard sedatives (Versed and Demerol), and performed the examination, which took, under the circumstances, twice as long as the usual time he required for such a procedure. The right side of the patient's colon was clean; the left was not.

This was the event that led to the arrest and conviction of Dr. Griffin and the revocation of his medical license—

though nothing occurred that gave any hint of the trouble to come. Certainly no one in the office could have suspected anything amiss from the demeanor of the patient, who rested in the procedure room for forty-five minutes after completion of the test and then sat in the waiting room nearly one hour more, in order, she explained, to get a prescription for her cold. She had nothing to say of any trouble to her boyfriend waiting outside to drive her home after the appointment.

Mrs. Jeffreys indeed gave numerous accounts of whom she first told, where she went, and what happened after the alleged assault by Dr. Griffin. She did not go to the police until February for various reasons, among them, she testified, because she couldn't find a station with a policewoman. As a black woman, she said further, she felt no one in authority would believe her. The first person she talked to, it seems, was a chiropractor, who informed Mrs. Jeffreys that her husband, an administrative court judge, would be greatly interested in her story—as the judge proved to be, with reason. After giving Mrs. Jeffreys the name of a civil attorney who could bring her case against the doctor, the judge co-signed a retainer agreement that would put him in line for a considerable chunk of any damages she might win.

At the doctor's trial in June 1996, numerous supporters appeared, including patients trying to raise defense funds for the now-bankrupt doctor. Along with them sat the defendant's wife, Kimberly Griffin, from whom he was separated, who listened to the charges in a state of consuming rage.

They were, indeed, stunning accusations. If Mrs. Jeffreys were to be believed, the defense attorney pointed out, Dr. Griffin had decided in the midst of his examination to place his tongue in a vagina that was swimming in fecal matter thanks to the condition in which the patient had arrived for the procedure. Liquid stool had begun flowing from her the moment he introduced the instrument. And he had chosen to do this in a thinly curtained room surrounded by staff workers four feet away, a room in which his assistants could enter at any moment. In his career, Dr. Griffin had performed close to 9,000 colonoscopies and endoscopies without ever having shown such proclivities—and now, the defense attorney asked, of all the women he might have violated he had decided to commit oral sodomy on one in this condition?

It was not the kind of question likely to concern prosecutor Linda Fairstein's Sex Crimes Unit, whose standard mode it was to try to establish a pattern of offenses. That was the function of the toll-free number calling on the doctor's patients to come forward—and come forward a number of women callers did, all of them with information Assistant District Attorney Bridget Fleming found highly significant.

Three women had called her to report that they had been given more sedation than they expected, prosecutor Fleming informed the trial judge, Marcy L. Kahn. Another woman had called to say she had awakened from the colonoscopy to find her hair mussed and wondered if that might be worth looking into. The assistant DA also brought word from a woman who called to say she had woken up in a room different from the one in which she'd had the procedure. Another one remembered that Dr. Griffin had given her a breast exam, and she wondered whether that was appropriate. Another called to report her discovery, after awakening from a procedure, that one of her earrings was missing. There were one or two more reports along these lines, in addition to one about a woman patient suffering from low blood sugar, who claimed the doctor had an affair with her and had bought her a dress. Each day brought new claims against the doctor. Assistant DA Fleming made frequent reference to the fact that he was a white man—a powerful white doctor whose high status intensified his victims' fear and sense of helplessness.

In her effort to portray the defendant as a liar, prosecutor Fleming one day asserted in court that she could find no such AIDS clinic as the one the doctor said he donated his services to on Fire Island, New York. The prosecutor referred here to the doctor's testimony on direct examination. With the rapid spread of AIDS in the mid-1980s and nobody knowing exactly what was happening, some physicians were reluctant to do endoscopies on HIV patients with gastrointestinal disease, he told the court. There was a fear that the HIV agent would spread. But Griffin had become something of an authority on one intestinal parasite found in AIDS patients, and because he had no reluctance to test and treat HIV patients with gastrointestinal disease, he became associated with the Gay Men's Health Crisis Center. He was on its list of recommended physicians and donated two or three hours of his time each week. He also donated two weekends and a full week to the Lindsey Clinic on Fire Island.

It was prosecutor Fleming's contention that no such clinic existed. In short, as far as the People were concerned, the doctor's testimony about his donated medical service was a fabrication. She had investigated—looked in the phone book, the paper, and various other places—she had even consulted a friend who lived in that community, the prosecutor informed the judge.

Enraged, defense attorney Gerald Shargel demanded the opportunity to present outside witnesses who would testify about the clinic, which did in fact exist. He had to correct the strong impression Assistant DA Fleming had left with the jury that the doctor lied about his service—this was an emotional issue—and for this he needed the witnesses. It was not enough to allow the doctor to provide the address. No such

witnesses would be necessary, Judge Kahn ruled, nor did she have the slightest reason to doubt the prosecutor had made her comments in good faith, a judgment Marcy Kahn was to make quite often in the course of this trial.

No claim would be more useful to the prosecution's case than the one the doctor had himself helped to engender, if inadvertently. Three and a half months after the alleged assault, Christine Jeffreys had arrived at the doctor's office wearing a huge wig and swaddled in a very large gold lamé raincoat. Under that coat, unknown to the doctor, was a tape recorder supplied by the police. After a brief exchange of pleasantries, the visitor got to the point—the charge that the doctor had sodomized her. She wanted to get something off her chest, she told him, and did he remember when she asked him to stop doing what he was doing?

DOCTOR: Doing what?

MRS. JEFFREYS: Uh . . . You had your mouth on my vagina and I did not—

DOCTOR: Oh, no, no, no, no.

MRS. JEFFREYS: No. Yes, you did.

DOCTOR: No, no, no, no.

MRS. JEFFREYS: Yes, you did.

DOCTOR: Absolutely not.

MRS. JEFFREYS: You did.

DOCTOR: No. Christine, no way.

MRS. JEFFREYS: You did. I asked you to stop.

DOCTOR: I did not.

MRS. JEFFREYS: You did. You did.

DOCTOR: Christine.

MRS. JEFFREYS: You know that you did. I asked you to stop. Dr. Griffin, after I asked you to stop you told me to turn over— no first you said, "I thought that's what you wanted me to do." And then you told me to turn over on my side and go back to sleep . . .

DOCTOR: No.

MRS. JEFFREYS: Yes.

It did not happen, the doctor said again.

"Yes, you did, " Mrs. Jeffreys told him. "I'm going to sit right here."

In the middle of all this, the tape recorder revealed, she began to talk about her civil suit against her landlord and to say she needed Dr. Griffin because he was acquainted with her case. She then returned to her first subject, the sexual as-

sault. She looked completely, unnervingly different from the patient he had known before, in her raincoat and huge wig, Dr. Griffin told the court.

He wanted to placate Mrs. Jeffreys, whom he viewed first and foremost as a patient, one he had treated for depression. He was not a man given to confrontation and certainly not with patients.

Dr. Griffin tried, the tape showed, to explain the effects of the sedatives Mrs. Jeffreys had been given. He also apologized to her for any perceived disrespect. He followed that piece of awkwardness, to his later regret, with a flustered academic effort to illustrate the effect the drug could have by telling her something that had *not* happened—that he had kissed her. The idea was that she would then think she remembered that and elaborate on the details, which would enable him to show her she was remembering details about something that had never happened.

Had he been a quicker thinker, he said at his trial, he would have picked a better example—something like, "Don't you remember me in a clown's suit halfway through the procedure?"

His sole purpose that night, he told the court, was to appease the combative patient he now saw before him—a woman he had treated for depression, now hurling shocking and incomprehensible charges and one, above all, whose next move he could not predict. She might run to the waiting room packed with patients and make a scene there, he thought. Fearing that, he focused all his energies on calming her and getting her out of his office.

Christine Jeffreys in fact had no intention of leaving the office just yet. Her hidden tape recorder rolling, she declared that she needed to know "that will not happen again."

"Nothing will ever happen again," the doctor replied.

"And will you apologize for doing that to me?"

"I apologize for doing anything to you."

The doctor repeated, again, "I never meant to do anything to hurt you at all."

"Okay, now good. Thank you."

The doctor then asked whether her stomach would now be better. She did not know, Mrs. Jeffreys replied. He had apologized, but she didn't know if she was accepting his apology.

"There was never any disrespect meant toward you at all."

"Okay."

"Under any circumstances."

Before she left, Mrs. Jeffreys again raised the problems she was having with her lawsuit.

That night, Griffin sat in his office angry and apprehensive, thinking about the patient who had made this accusation. All the years he had treated her, Christine Jeffreys had

had but one preoccupation he knew of, and that was her hope of prevailing in her civil suit. He set about composing a self-protective note that reflected the spirit, if not the exact detail, of the meeting with her. He wrote, for example, that he had told his accuser that she should see a psychiatrist. This he had in fact done a few months earlier, but not at this encounter, as the tape recording would show. On such grounds, Linda Fairstein's office decided to charge him with another felony: falsification of business records.

There would be, besides oral sodomy, an additional charge of sex abuse, this as a result of Mrs. Jeffreys's complaint that while performing her colonoscopy, he touched her vagina with his hand.

On the stand, Mrs. Jeffreys told of the apprehension she had felt about testifying and the strength she had needed to endure the ordeal. She could have spared herself much of her apprehension. As became clear early in the proceedings, the complaining witness had nothing to fear in this courtroom, where she received singular protection from any line of questioning that might raise doubts about her credibility.

In pretrial colloquies, the defense had outlined the issues on which it planned to cross-examine Mrs. Jeffreys, to include, among other issues, her history of filing civil suits and various questions about the truthfulness of her testimony in these.

It was hard enough, an angry prosecutor argued, for

women to come forward with these charges. "If they are going to get beat up on things that don't have any relevance to the case, they are not going to come forward. " She suggested the judge think of the policy perspective.

"It's an outrage, Your Honor, that because a woman was sexually assaulted by her doctor, that she had to go through this kind of treatment."

Judge Kahn needed no persuasion, having, as she clearly did, a policy of her own in these matters. Accordingly, she prohibited the defense from raising instances of the complainant's alleged perjury in the civil case against her landlord and also in her testimony against the doctor before the Office of Professional and Medical Conduct. The defense could not raise her prior meritless litigations, her history of financial trouble, her string of bounced checks, nor could the jury know the millions she was asking in her suit against the doctor—all issues that could establish motive and a willingness to lie for financial gain.

Explaining her rulings, Judge Kahn numerous times cited her belief, which coincided with that of the prosecutor—namely, that victims of sex crimes merit special protection if others are to be encouraged to come forward. Mrs. Jeffreys had come forward with a claim of sexual victimization. Therefore, the judge announced, she would not allow the defense to ask questions about her prior perjured testimony "to avoid harassment of the witness." It was a phrase she would repeat frequently in the course of her rulings. She wanted to avoid, declared the judge, "an atmosphere where someone who says she has suffered a sexual offense does not feel too intimidated to come forward and tell a jury about it."

If the complaining witness felt intimidated, it was well concealed. At one point, Mrs. Jeffreys called the defense attorney "slime" within earshot of the jury, a fact the attorney called to the judge's attention. Requesting that Mrs. Jeffreys not repeat this behavior, Judge Kahn assured her she understood the stress that must burden a witness in such a case.

The defense counsel all the while continued battling the limits imposed on his cross-examination of Mrs. Jeffreys. The judge was making it impossible to have any meaningful confrontation with the witness, the infuriated defense attorney argued.

Prosecutor Fleming had no such complaints. The Assistant DA indeed introduced one unsubstantiated story after another alleging various acts of lewd misconduct by Dr. Griffin. One such story, about the doctor's masturbating in front of a patient, was finally too much for Judge Kahn, who warned the prosecutor that she could not bring this one up before the jury. Nonetheless, she proceeded to do just that while cross-examining Dr. Griffin.

Here the judge stopped her short, and the defense called

for a mistrial. She would not declare a mistrial, Judge Kahn decided. It was enough, she concluded, that she had instructed the jury to disregard the inflammatory reference to masturbation, which the judge said was "a buzz word." And there would be no mistrial because, the judge once again found, the prosecutor's offense had been made in good faith.

No other witness but Mrs. Jeffreys appeared in court to say that the physician had ever molested her. On the witness stand, she told of the suffering and injury she had sustained as a result of the doctor's act—details also itemized in the bill of particulars filed in her civil lawsuit against him. She had sworn to those claims, had she not? the defense asked. She had, Mrs. Jeffreys agreed. The defense attorney then proceeded to query her about the claims filed in the civil suit.

Because of the crime committed against her in the doctor's office, "You had difficulty participating in a formalized dance program, right?"

Yes, she answered, and she had problems with her social life. She also now declined invitations for social events such as dining out.

"You haven't been dining out?" attorney Shargel asked.

"On occasion, I have not."

"You have not gone to the movies because of what occurred?"

"On occasion, I have not. Except dates to the movies, because of what has happened to me, yes."

Because of what happened to her she had not gone to the beach?

"Oh, I used to frequent the beach, but now I don't because of what has happened to me."

She also watched too much television as a result of what the doctor had done, the jury learned, and she had gained twenty pounds—while also losing her appetite.

The day Dr. Griffin was alleged to have committed the crime, was, as it happened, his birthday. For this occasion, his office manager testified, the staff had prepared a surprise party. Asked, on the stand, how old he was that day, the doctor replied, "I would have been forty."

It was an oddly worded answer but clear to at least one person in the courtroom. The doctor's patient, Marilyn Lasker, whose aged mother Dr. Griffin had treated with a degree of care far beyond the call of duty, reflected, "In his mind, life ended that day."

She and her husband, Judge Arthur Lasker, attended the trial every day. In the long grim months before he went on trial, Dr. Griffin kept a notebook record of everyone, patients or colleagues, who called to offer support or just to say hello. Many did, and there were also those doctor friends who turned away. When the defense committee asked for a contribution, one physician Dr. Griffin had gone out of his way to befriend sent $10. This he needed no notebook to remember.

On June 20, 1996, the jury came in with a guilty verdict. The doctor stood convicted of the charge of sodomy in the first degree and of altering business records. He was acquitted of the one count of sexual abuse, brought on the basis of Mrs. Jeffreys's claim the defendant's hand touched her vagina during the colonoscopy.

With the sentencing set for late July, Dr. Griffin's anguished band of patients and other supporters, led by Judge Arthur Lasker, set about collecting funds to pay for the appeal. The money came in dribs and drabs and also in large sums. One patient long employed at Columbia University cashed in her retirement fund.

The appellate attorney recommended to Dr. Griffin was Harvey Stone, whose first act was to go to the scene where the crime was supposed to have taken place, to look at the physical arrangements and the examining room, to estimate how plausible it was that the crimes charged could have taken place in these circumstances. During the trial, the defense attorney had asked that the jurors be allowed to do the same, a request Judge Kahn refused.

At the now desolate medical office, Stone found Dr. Griffin seated at a desk, one side of his face distorted and drooping—the effects, the doctor calmly told him, of an attack of Bell's palsy, which he had never had before and could be triggered by extreme anxiety. The symptom would soon pass, though not its cause. With his conviction, he now faced a mandatory sentence of at least two years. And there was little doubt the district attorney would be asking for more.

At the sentencing hearing, Assistant DA Fleming argued that it was true that the doctor's patients trusted him and that they had sent remarkable letters of support—but that it was this very fact that should be considered proof of the exceptional heinousness of his crime. The defendant engendered great trust in his patients, and Mrs. Jeffreys had trusted him. "She had no suspicion, your honor, on January 13 of 1995, that she was going to wake up during the procedure while he was performing oral sex on her and that her life would be changed forever by the shocking nature of that crime." This was, reiterated the prosecutor, a crime so horrifying it would live with Mrs. Jeffreys forever. Moreover, the prosecutor argued, the defendant continued to protest his innocence, which clearly showed a lack of remorse and an effort to avoid taking responsibility. Prosecutor Fleming cited the strength of the case against the doctor and the reports the DA's office had gathered from callers to the toll-free number, an address in which she did not neglect to mention the missing earring.

Mrs. Jeffreys delivered a statement of her own, which she began by thanking God for giving her strength to endure the court ordeal. She now faced great struggles getting herself to see physicians—her entire life had been transformed, she told the court. "There has not been a quiet day for me since January 13 up until this day and it's not going to end today. Because he is being sentenced for something he did is not going to end for me today. It is going to continue and continue and continue. This type of abuse never disappears, it remains."

She was outraged, she said, turning to the doctor: "To continue to be in denial for what you did, to continue to sit here in this courtroom and say you want to appeal."

Judge Kahn instructed her to direct her comments to the bench, and Mrs. Jeffreys continued. She wanted an example set. A lot of women didn't have the courage to come forward and say what happened, but she had. "It was a lot of pain for me. My family still go through a lot of stress. I still go through a lot of stress." The doctor had been convicted. "And he should be punished to the maximum for what he did."

Judge Kahn asked the doctor to stand while she imposed sentence, to come after a statement of her own, whose main themes echoed those of the prosecutor. Like the prosecutor, Judge Kahn saw in the testaments from his patients about the doctor's devoted care and his integrity all the more proof of the terrible nature of his assault. He had, the judge said, "held himself out as a healer and protector." His crime was therefore particularly heinous. "It involves a betrayal of trust as well as an act of cowardly violence."

Judge Kahn observed that his patients praised him for his exemplary clinical and diagnostic skills. "They applaud him for taking on the hopeless cases and turning them around. Many people believe he has saved their lives or the lives of their loved ones and have expressed personal devastation at the prospect of losing him as their doctor."

Because of this, people put their trust and welfare in him, and, the judge charged, he had encouraged them to do so. "He felt he did not have to follow the rules—that he could get away with anything. A violation of another human being's personhood," said the judge, left scars that could last a lifetime. "It is one of the most horrible experiences one can undergo physically and emotionally." She was aware, the judge said, that it was his first offense. She was also aware that he continued to deny his guilt and expressed no remorse.

His crime, Judge Kahn informed him, was designated a B violent felony precisely because it was a serious violent crime.

The judge did not give Dr. Griffin the maximum sentence permitted by law, as Mrs. Jeffreys wished, or the four to twelve years the prosecutor asked. She instead sentenced him to three and a third years to ten years in state prison, to begin the following Monday morning. This would give the defense time to seek a stay of the sentence and bail pending appeal from the Appellate Division, though, Judge Kahn observed, she could think of no issues in this trial that would warrant reversal on appeal. She then issued an order of protection for Christine Jeffreys.

Appellate attorney Harvey Stone sat in the back of the courtroom taking it all in. The sentencing over, he instructed Dr. Griffin to wait downstairs for him while he raced to the appellate court to deliver a brief describing the arguments for appeal. These were sufficiently compelling to persuade the sitting justice, Gustav Rosenberger, who granted a stay and an order that the doctor remain free on bail pending appeal. Immediately thereafter, Judge Kahn moved to have Dr. Griffin certified as a sex offender. The grant of a stay, she ruled, did not exempt him from the requirement to register as a sex offender.

Stone, the former chief of the Appeals Division of the U.S. Attorney's office for the Eastern District of New York, got to work on the appeal brief, a labor of many weeks and long nights. Shargel's voluminous notes helped. Frustrated at the limits put on his cross-examination, confounded at the judge's rulings favoring the prosecution and her efforts to protect the complainant from stress, the defense attorney had carefully preserved all of it for the record.

In April 1998, a year and a half after the verdict, the appellate court reversed Dr. Griffin's conviction. It was a rare victory in a state supreme court not given to reversals in criminal cases. Fewer than 4 percent of convictions appealed were, like this one, thrown out on all counts. In their ruling, the justices found, among other reasons for reversal, that the trial judge had unreasonably curtailed defense cross-examination of the complainant. They pointed out that the rape shield law, which severely restricts efforts to impeach a complainant with questions about prior sexual history, did not mean that alleged sex crime victims could be protected against all other forms of impeachment, including those tending to show hostility or monetary incentive to fabricate. The majority also found that the prosecutor's reference to the doctor's masturbating in front of a patient was intentional misconduct, poisonous in its impact on the jury.

Even so, Dr. Griffin still faced the prospect of a retrial.

Appalled by everything about the prosecution, as the distinct edge of rage in his appellate brief clearly showed, Stone now undertook an effort to dissuade Linda Fairstein and the Manhattan District Attorney's office from mounting another trial. At a meeting with the Manhattan DA's chief assistant, which Assistant DA Fleming also attended, Stone offered all the arguments for not mounting another trial, chief among them the fact that the doctor was innocent of the charges. He offered another lie detector test, conscious that, although they were inadmissible in court, law enforcement relied heavily on such tests. Stone cited the one that had been administered by one of the best-known, most reputable polygraphers in the business, which the doctor had passed with flying colors. If this were not enough, the DA's office could pick a polygrapher of its choice.

All in vain. The tenor of the response left little doubt that the DA's office was bent on a retrial.

Griffin now got a new trial attorney, Paul Callan, former deputy chief of homicide in the Brooklyn District Attorney's office. Callan was worried. The statistics told the story. Ninety percent of retried cases ended in conviction. He wanted Dr. Griffin to consider that fact in the event that some reasonable plea deal were offered. Callan accordingly met with Linda Fairstein and with Bridget Fleming and did get an offer of a deal: probation for the doctor in exchange for some admission of guilt on a sex charge.

The proposal was out of the question, the doctor told Callan, who warned him again he faced a high risk of conviction. He had committed no such crime, Patrick Griffin said, and he would take no such plea.

At the second trial, in April 2000, Bridget Fleming again presented the People's case against Patrick Griffin. Assistant

DA Fleming, who had taken a pounding in the app
court's stinging majority decision, had lost none o
ardor. It was nonetheless clear that this would be a tria
different from the first one in crucial ways, foremost a
them the tone and the rulings emanating from the
Unpreoccupied with imperatives like the need to enc
rape victims to come forward, Judge Jeffrey Atlas af
the defense counsel the standard rights of cross-exami
He also precluded any attempt to inject the race of th
plaining witness, as prosecutor Fleming had done
first trial.

Mrs. Jeffreys was as impassioned an accuser as
if also a more uneasy one under Callan's relentles
dial cross-examination. A specialist in physician ma
cases, he had learned to tread carefully when dealing
leged victims, often the object of juries' sympathies.
this jury detailed explanations of the effects of the c
ministered to Mrs. Jeffreys the morning of the colc
Demerol and Versed were known to produce mer
and sexual fantasy, precisely the reason that women
were not given Versed, he told the jurors. Its power
would wipe out the memory of the birth.

With the trial ended and the jury verdict due, I
went to church to say a prayer and then returned
where he waited, head bowed. He did not have lc

before the jurors filed in, looking straight at him, some smiling. When the foreman announced his acquittal, the doctor wept. There were tears too in the eyes of some of the jurors, whose views of the prosecutors' case the judge evidently shared. After the trial, Judge Atlas asked Callan why the doctor hadn't waived a jury trial. "I would have had your client acquitted two days ago," the judge told him.

Immediately after his conviction, the Office of Professional and Medical Conduct had stripped Dr. Griffin of his medical license. Now, uncertainly gathering the shards of a career, the doctor had no immediate plans. It would take more than a license to restore the world lost to him when the District Attorney's Sex Crimes Unit descended.

Griffin began writing letters seeking employment. He received few answers. When a former colleague who had read about his trials and exoneration called with an offer of a position doing research on new gastrointestinal drugs, Dr. Griffin was more than willing. The job was interesting, the pay good. As the year wore on, he immersed himself more and more in his new work, free of association with trials and terror.

When he might resume his career as a doctor, he had no idea, he told anyone who asked—he had, as they say, no plans. At the large, boisterous victory celebration held in a friendly Manhattan pub after the doctor's acquittal, his patients crowded around, raising joyful toasts. They spoke of

his skill, of how kindly and well he had treated them, of the bracing optimism that had helped them and lifted their hearts, and how good it would be to see him in his office again. None of them knew how slight the chance was that they would ever do so.

The Amiraults, Part Four

Few people hearing Justice Fried's assertions that there was nothing unusual in charges like those against the Amiraults—of children seduced in mass orgies, violated by caretakers dressed as clowns, in magic rooms—can have failed to note the strangeness of the comment. There can have been few people in that courtroom unaware that the signal feature of prosecutions like this was the extraordinary nature of the accusations. Trials like those of the McMartins and Kelly Michaels had spawned phenomenal accusations—phenomenal, and also almost exactly the same everywhere they were held. Residents of Massachusetts, stunned by revelations about animals tortured, about death threats, big cameras, and secret rooms in the Amiraults' school, could not have known in just how many parts of the country prosecutors had uncovered the same crimes, virtually identical in all their colorful detail—and not surprisingly, since investigators interrogating children in prosecutions across the country shaped their questions around the same list of pedophilic tricks and abuse symptoms.

In the brutalities of actual child abuse that courts see every day, there are no clowns, no elephants, no butchered bluebirds or magic rooms. The charges are plain, stark violation without frills. In these, children don't talk about molestation in hot air balloons or visits from robots, about magic potions, or being forced to drink urine or eat excrement—details that emerged again and again in cases from New Jersey to California.

The general tone of Fried's questions from the bench was not encouraging. The Amiraults left the hearing downcast, despite their attorneys' assurances that it was hard to tell how the court would decide on the basis of the oral argument. The attorneys walked away, to be sure, more downcast than the family. They knew, in ways the Amiraults and the McGonagles did not, the near impossibility of keeping Cheryl from prison, not to mention freedom for Gerald, if the Supreme Judicial Court ruled against them now.

Gerald's case, and that of Violet and Cheryl, had taken separate legal tracks, but there was no separating Gerald's prospects from the court rulings on Cheryl. It had long been decided that the attorneys would move ahead with Cheryl's appeal in the expectation that a favorable result there would carry over to Gerald.

As she had long done, Cheryl found sustenance in work. In 1999, while awaiting the decision that would determine whether she was to be returned to Framingham, she went to work at John Hancock Financial Services, beginning as an office temporary, and was soon after hired full time. She had no idea whether her employers knew who she was, nor did she ask.

In August 1999, a unanimous Supreme Judicial Court overturned Justice Borenstein's ruling granting Cheryl a new trial. Justice Fried had a few months earlier suddenly left the court. The decision, which carried the name of Chief Justice Herbert P. Wilkins, made Cheryl's return to prison a virtual certainty, probably within a month. The decision was a kind of death blow to Gerald's hopes for a successful state appeal.

The ruling exhilarated a core of faithful believers in the case against the Amiraults, among them Wendy Murphy, frequent commentator on child advocacy issues, who proclaimed, "Stick a fork in them. They're done."

The opinion was a telling document as much for what the justices left out as for what they put in. The justices— Herbert P. Wilkins, Margaret H. Marshall, John Greaney,

Ruth Abrams, Neil L. Lynch, and Roderick L. Ireland—confined themselves mainly to their argument that the issue of tainted evidence was not new, that it had been presented at the original trial, and that the jury had believed the children anyway. It was the court's view that these were matters of greater significance than the issues uncovered by Justice Borenstein, more important than the origins of the testimony that had led inexorably to the Amiraults' convictions.

———

If, as the opinion made clear, Justice Borenstein's findings of fact had not swayed the justices, it had nevertheless had a serious impact on public perceptions of the case. This voluminous work, detailed, scholarly, and infused with controlled rage, had been compiled not by the Amiraults' attorneys or other supporters but by a highly respected Superior Court judge appointed by the court.

Isaac Borenstein's lengthy exposure to the evidence in the Amirault case had had its impact on him as well. So exercised did he become in the course of daily immersion in the prosecutors' evidence that he could barely sleep. When he received news of the Supreme Judicial Court's decision reinstating Cheryl's conviction, the furious justice ordered the state prosecutor, the Amiraults, and their attorneys to appear

before him in open court. The news inspired fevered speculation as to what he intended. In the event, Martha Coakley,
the new Middlesex County district attorney, made clear her
position that the judge could not compel her appearance.
Whatever Justice Borenstein had in mind, few people would
ever learn. Higher authorities in the Superior Court advised
him that it might be best to cancel the order.

Less than two weeks later, there would be clear evidence
that, the Supreme Judicial Court notwithstanding, opinion
on the Amirault case had taken a significant turn. The opinion of the Massachusetts Lawyers Weekly became a news
story in itself, carried on the wires, the airwaves, and in the
Boston papers. There was good reason for the interest in this
story. Never before in the twenty-seven-year history of the
weekly had it taken direct issue with or sharply criticized any
ruling by the state's highest court. The journal's editor, Paul
M. Martinek, noted that it was all too easy to criticize the
court on a particular ruling, and so the journal had always
avoided editorializing. But the editors were now moved to
break precedent because, Martinek explained, the Supreme
Judicial Court had rendered a decision that reflected shame-
fully on the Massachusetts judicial system of which he and
his colleagues had always been proud.

The editorial, titled "Travesty of Justice," declared, "In six
different decisions in the Amirault cases the SJC has seemed

determined to defend the prosecutors and insist that these defendants belong behind bars. Virtually scoffing at any possibility that an injustice may have been done the justices have been unyielding in their refusal to let a new trial take place." Further: "The prosecutors here seem unwilling to admit any possibility that they might have sent innocent people to jail for crimes that never occurred. Yes, confrontation rights were violated. Yes, investigation tactics were unduly suggestive. . . . But, according to prosecutors, the jurors believed the children and that's all that matters."

There was more from other Massachusetts papers. The Christian Science Monitor noted that this was "the second time in two years the court refused to correct . . . a prosecution that should never have been brought."

With Cheryl's rearrest imminent, James Sultan, now sole attorney for the Amiraults, filed a petititon to reconsider. As expected, the court rejected it.

Cheryl prepared herself for prison again. The prospect of return to Framingham seemed at once harder and easier now that she was without her mother—but mostly harder, the family thought, as she did herself. She would not now have to worry about her mother's frailty, the trouble she had keeping pace. Still, frail though she was, Violet had been Cheryl's strength in prison and out of it. How it would be alone in Framingham now, she could not think.

She heard conjectures, meant as comfort, that she could probably win early parole, perhaps in a year or less. Cheryl knew nevertheless, as her attorneys did, that once she was inside, there were no guarantees. She would not get out for a long time.

As James Sultan began looking for ways to prevent Cheryl's return to prison, help came from an unexpected quarter: Harvard Law professor Charles Ogletree, a former public defender and head of Harvard's Criminal Justice Institute, offered help. He could not stand back and watch this struggle any longer, announced Ogletree, the sole member of Harvard's otherwise much quoted faculty prepared to take public notice of this unavoidably noticeable case reeking and smoldering in the neighborhood.

Ogletree had influence and connections not available to James Sultan, among them a friendly relationship with the newly elected DA, Martha Coakley. Coakley had not been around for the trials of the Amiraults, but the new head of the Middlesex County DA's office would soon prove to be a faithful representative of the reigning political culture, not least with regard to the Amirault case.

Still, with Ogletree's help, Sultan got the DA to agree to a motion revising Cheryl's sentence to time served. The motion was approved by a Superior Court judge and the deal done: Cheryl would not be forced to return to prison. The victory was not without its costs—among these the end of any lingering hope that the DA might give Gerald similar consideration. That hope, to be sure, had always been slender. Justice Robert Barton was not alone in noting, years before, "They're going to do everything to hold on to him"— an accurate prediction, as Coakley's pronouncements now made abundantly clear.

Confronted with reporters' questions about Gerald's prospects now that Cheryl had been released, the DA explained that the two cases had nothing to do with one another, itself a proposition that startled more than a few journalists. In her further explanations, DA Coakley laid the groundwork for the role the prosecutors now assigned Gerald: that of the family master criminal who had dragged the hapless women along. The prosecutor's reasons for this emphasis would soon become quite clear.

"There are," Coakley told reporters, "fewer female sex offenders. But where there are women involved, there is often a primary male offender involved." It was apparently her contention that when women were involved in such crimes along with a male, the women were to be considered less culpable, because the male was the primary offender. In short, Gerald was the primary offender.

Every comment now issuing from District Attorney Coakley bore out what everyone schooled in the facts of this story had always known: that the prosecutors would never let go of Gerald Amirault, the symbol of their victorious case. They would fight his release with all the tenacity and passion available to them. Those who doubted had only to listen, now, to Coakley's repeated announcements that the agreement freeing Cheryl had no impact whatever on Gerald's status and would have none in the future.

The DA's preoccupation with this issue revealed itself early in the negotiations with James Sultan. Before agreeing to free Cheryl, Coakley asked Sultan to make a remarkable pledge. Specifically, the DA wanted Sultan to promise that if she agreed to Cheryl's release, he would cease representing Gerald and would take no part in any further legal effort on his behalf.

It was apparently the prosecutor's view that with Sultan gone—Sultan, whose command of every aspect of the case was unrivaled—Gerald Amirault's further efforts to win his freedom would be crippled, if not entirely undone. Coakley might not have made such a request—though about such things it is impossible to know—had she understood anything about Sultan or the seven years and countless hours, many of them unpaid, he had spent trying to free the Amiraults.

Having refused to accommodate Coakley in this, Sultan next dealt with certain other of the DA's concerns, evident in the clauses of a special agreement she had drawn up. In these, Cheryl would forswear all appearances on television— a prohibition that made news in all quarters of the media, not least the television news. For their part, print journalists could hardly have failed to notice what this said about where the DA ranked their importance.

Not entirely blind to appearances, Coakley took the precaution of making the restriction a mutual agreement of sorts and not legally binding, which could not obscure the fact that a person whose hopes for freedom rested with the DA could hardly be said to have had a choice in the matter. The district attorney's letter of agreement put the matter clearly:

> *We have agreed, in addition to any conditions of probation, that I, on behalf of the Commonwealth and Cheryl Amirault LeFave, on behalf of herself, will not discuss in television interviews or before television cameras, either live or for film footage.*
>
> *Accordingly, both the Commonwealth and Cheryl Amirault LeFave agree that as to the facts and circumstances of the case, the judicial proceedings surrounding the case and the negotiations relating to the resolution of this motion to revise and revoke, we will not comment further before television media for the*

*duration of Cheryl Amirault LeFave's probation, which
will run until October of 2009.*

Assistant DA Lynn Rooney explained that the stipulation against television was warranted in order that innocent children and their parents, who had suffered so much at the hands of the Amiraults, would not have to be pained further by having to hear Cheryl arguing her innocence on television. Why they would suffer less hearing Cheryl argue the Amiraults' innocence in radio interviews, on which there were no constraints, neither Rooney nor anyone else in the DA's office ventured to explain. The no-television proscription brought a flood of mockery from local press commentators about what the DA might be trying to hide, along with cartoons and acid jokes about where Cheryl could and could not be heard.

There was, to be sure, a reason for the no-television proscription that had little to do with the suffering of the innocent children and much to do with the prosecutors' target political audience. The prosecutors minded any time Cheryl or any other of the Amiraults gave interviews, whether to the print press or radio or any other sector of the media—but what they minded most of all was an Amirault interview on television. The audience that television reached was not only huge; it was also the most emotionally accessible one.

The Amiraults' prosecutors had by now lost considerable ground in the war for public opinion and had no intention of losing more if they could help it. One sector of the public was particularly important—that vast audience not normally exposed to opinions of the educated elite, who didn't know about Justice Borenstein's investigation or law journal editorials. This was the audience that got its news from television, that could be expected to feel empathy for the parents in wigs and dark glasses talking about their children's suffering, that would detest the abusers of children and embrace the prosecutors who had put them away. The DA had her reasons for not wanting Cheryl's tear-streaked face on TV screens—Cheryl asserting her innocence, talking about her mother and her brother and the years all of them had lost to prison over crimes that had never taken place.

There were other conditions for her release, these legally binding. They included ten years' probation, during which time she would be forbidden contact with any child under the age of sixteen. Nothing, however, would approach the weight of the requirement regarding her future legal efforts. As a condition of her release Cheryl had to renounce all future appeals and court efforts to overturn her conviction. This she agreed to with anguish, but also with little doubt that it was the thing to do. Gerald was still in prison. His future appeals—and vindication—must stand for hers. Her deceased mother, Violet, was now the only Amirault who required no future effort to clear her name. The Supreme Judicial Court could not legally overturn Justice Borenstein's ruling posthumously exonerating her.

With the assurance that Cheryl would remain free, Gerald felt almost as exhilarated as the day Judge Barton first overturned the women's convictions. He was now finally shed of the fears for them he carried through the years his mother and sister were in prison. Despite assurances from Violet and from his sister, and from Patti and Phil and Mary, who had regularly visited them, he had been haunted by worries over their safety. The abiding faith he had in Violet's strength was small comfort during the cold dawn hours he had spent envisioning her surrounded by criminals and addicts, the noise, the cellmates.

All worries about his own situation he kept strictly to himself when communicating with Violet and Cheryl. "Everything is all right, I'm fine," was his standard report to his mother and sister. He had gone to this or that class, or taken part in some activity, got a letter, wrote a letter, received a visitor.

This censorship did not, of course, extend to his reports to Patti. She was the one who heard his fears, his anger over the lack of progress in his case—the one he lashed out at from time to time at what he perceived as some missed chance, something that had not been done that could have

been. After these outbursts there came, invariably, a quick apology and, after he hung up, the tortured thoughts about the burdens she had been left to carry: the children to raise, the bills that could barely be met, the endless work hours, and her heaviest duty, sustaining him.

Patti Amirault seldom concerned herself with Gerald's outbursts, which were, in any case, infrequent. She had matters more pressing on her mind, most of them worries about the children and about money, and surrounding these, a fog of anxiety with her so long she had become accustomed to it. It required effort to remember there had been a time when she felt otherwise, an effort she had neither time nor inclination to make often. It was, anyway, beside the point. Now was the time she lived in.

Her memories of the life that was before, when she sought them, were altogether too clear. She sometimes thought back to the long days watching Gerald trim his lawn, a job he loved, with the children trailing after him. Just after he had been taken off to prison, it came to her as she sat, exhausted, how much her husband had always done around the house, much more than she did—diapering and laundry and dishes, everything. It was an odd thing to be thinking about under the circumstances, but it stayed with her.

Nowadays she could deal with everything, every emergency. It helped to have her mother and father, generous

with what little money they had, and to have her large family, and their dinners and holiday celebrations—their efforts to cheer her. It helped to take on the role of ultimate activities chauffeur. She managed somehow, between her multiple jobs, to drive her son around to his team games—to this tournament or that, in Massachusetts or Canada, it hardly mattered. It had to be done, and she adored doing it and reporting it all to Gerald. It had to be done, too, because in the unending busyness, she had found her way of coping.

Still, her anxieties took their toll, with mysterious pains, swelling of the neck that came and went, and other attacks for which no organic cause could be found. When the children were small and ten minutes late coming home, she was a wreck, and nothing she told herself about how ridiculous she was being could lessen her fears. Now the children were no longer children—the girls were grown up, and P.J. was a teenager—the fears for them had somewhat diminished. Now Patti began to worry about her son's state of mind and inattention in school.

A somber boy of few words, P.J. had appeared at every court hearing involving the three Amiraults, and they had been many. In his seventeenth year, he would attend another one. With Cheryl freed in October 1999, James Sultan and his law partner, Charles Rankin, pondered the next steps for Gerald. They were not alone. Some years earlier, the Ami-

rault case had attracted the attention of a prominent Boston attorney, Harvey Silverglate, who soon began donating time behind the scenes. Silverglate offered counsel, helped devise strategy, found reasons for optimism evident to no one else, and came up with another route to pursue when every last recourse seemed exhausted. Silverglate had conceived the strategy that led to the fact-finding hearings conducted by Justice Borenstein. Now, Silverglate, Sultan, and Rankin decided that the most promising possibility for Gerald was a petition for commutation by the governor of the Commonwealth of Massachusetts.

This was more than just another roll of the dice. Early in 2000, newly elected Republican governor Paul Cellucci, who had just defeated the heavily favored Democratic candidate, Amirault prosecutor Scott Harshbarger, appeared on a radio call-in show. He was asked what he thought about the Amirault case, and Gerald's prospects in particular. By way of reply, the governor murmured that it was his view that Gerald Amirault had not received justice. Listening in his car, Silverglate wondered if he could actually have heard this or perhaps had only imagined it.

The question sufficed to send Sultan and Silverglate eagerly racing for copies of the studio tape, which did reveal the governor's expressing doubts about whether Gerald Amirault had received justice.

Sultan immediately began preparing a commutation petition to be filed with Cellucci's office. A lengthy history of the case, which was supposed to concern only Gerald and avoid focus on issues of guilt or innocence, was filed in April 2000. That the petition, which came complete with exhibits that included Justice Isaac Borenstein's scathing Findings of Fact, ensured that the question of guilt or innocence would commend itself to the attention of the Governor's Advisory Board on Pardons and Paroles, which recommends approval or denial of commutation appeals.

It was unlikely, to be sure, that there could be any member of the board by now unaware of the notoriety attaching to the Amirault prosecutions. Even so, it came as something of a shock to the Amirault attorneys, albeit a pleasant one, to learn that the board had set a hearing date for September, just a few months off. The board rarely provided hearings in answer to requests for commutation or parole. Most petitions to the Governor's Board were denied, no meetings required.

On September 20, police guards escorted Gerald to a small Boston hearing room soon to be crowded with relatives, friends, and other interested parties. The last imprisoned member of the Amirault family was permitted a suit and tie for this occasion, and an occasion it was, there could be no doubt. This prisoner and his attorneys knew how few commutation appeals were granted.

Filing in next came Gerald's wife and children, the Mc-
Gonagles, and the rest of the extended family, a quiet crowd
with an an air of slightly exhausted anticipation. They had
attended many hearings, awaited many decisions, always
wary of hope, always, invariably, uncontrollably hopeful.

Near them, just across a narrow aisle, sat another silent
contingent of spectators: the parents and other relatives of
the child witnesses who had testified against Violet, Cheryl,
and Gerald. Just one of those witnesses for the prosecution
sat amid the knot of Fells Acres parents. In her early twenties
now, the former nursery school pupil had come, like the parents, to express outrage at the prospect of commutation for
Gerald Amirault.

First would come certain procedural matters, instruc-
tions, introductions, ground rules, and a roster of other
speakers beginning with Gerald—Gerald who had only to
begin speaking to undo every shred of the calm formal-
ity with which these proceedings had begun. As he stood
to address the board—composed of three former prosecutors, a former state trooper, a former probation officer, and
a victim's representative—a great tide of emotion swept
the benches where the Amiraults sat. His daughters, Katie
and Gerrilyn, held on to one another and tried to stifle their
sobs. In the row ahead sat P.J., dry-eyed and impassive as
always.

Gerald had been in prison more than fourteen years,

most of them in segregation units. He had tried in all that time to figure out how this misery had come to him and his family and he had failed, Gerald told the board. He had no answers. He was not an expert. He asked now, he said, only for an end to the nightmare in which he and his family had lived for so many years. He asked also that the board not hold it against him that he refused to confess that he was guilty—that he refused now, as always—and that he would continue to do so. "I am absolutely innocent of all these charges."

Under exhausting questioning by a board member he readily conceded that he had entered no prison program for the rehabilitation of sex offenders all the years of his imprisonment. He was not, he explained, a sex offender.

He spoke as a man well aware of the dangers of this response, given the prevailing view within the corrections system that convicted offenders must accept guilt to be considered rehabilitated. Like his mother, Violet, and his sister, Gerald had not ceased to assert his innocence, whatever the cost to his hopes for parole.

On the list of those addressing the board this day were Gerald Amirault's wife, his son, P.J., and his two conspicuously handsome daughters—one a college senior of twenty-one, the other twenty and in her junior year. Their voices breaking, each described the father they had known as children and knew now—the father shut away but still at the center of their lives. In this suddenly airless room, there was now nothing but these voices raw with longing and grief. In the small hearing chamber, people fought back tears—or stared straight ahead with a trapped look. At the rear of the room, the briskly professional security officer who had thoroughly searched every visitor sat and wept.

Gerald's attorney, James Sultan, next rose to affirm his understanding that this hearing concerned only one issue: the question of commutation for Gerald, on the grounds that disparate punishment had been meted out for the same crimes. That disparity had been clear enough in the length of sentence given him as compared with the one given his mother and sister. Now, Sultan pointed out, there was the evidence of a still more glaring, and much more recent, inequity.

Last October, when her appeal was rejected and Cheryl faced returning to prison, a politically discomfiting prospect for the DA's office, Martha Coakley agreed to revise and revoke her sentence to time served. Yet today the DA adamantly opposed any such relief for Gerald. That, Sultan said, was the issue. He understood, of course, that the Board was not supposed to consider questions of guilt or innocence or the merits of the prosecution.

Everyone understood. And still there was no way to ignore the elephant in the living room: that huge body of opinion, legal and other, that now saw the case against the Amiraults as a sham built on accusations coaxed from children. No fewer than three lower court judges had declared it such.

In the end, it was the representative from the DA's office who would bring the elephant trundling in, to remind everyone of all that had made this case notorious. Notwithstanding the stricture against talk about guilt or innocence, which the board is not supposed to consider, Assistant DA Lynn Rooney launched into an impassioned address on just that subject, in which she described Gerald's crime and recited details of the children's testimony.

Here again was the magic room in which Gerald attacked the preschoolers while disguised as a clown; the story about Violet Amirault terrorizing children with threats that they would never see their parents again; and another darkly meandering one about Violet selecting certain children to be left behind while others went on field trips and how she had taken children from one classroom and put them in another.

The families had suffered pain beyond measure; the children were prone to obsessive-compulsive disorders and all manner of other disturbances, the assistant DA argued, and they needed closure. They would never have closure if Gerald went free. Above all, Gerald Amirault had not even found it in himself to confess to the crimes that had ravaged so many lives. If there were some acknowledgment that he committed the crimes, DA Rooney said, "the parents could begin to process this event."

Board member John Kivlan brought Rooney back to the issue at hand: the matter of different punishments for the same crimes. Had the DA not agreed last October to revise and revoke Cheryl Amirault's sentence? And if that were so, why should Gerald not be treated the same? Kivlan asked.

The importance of Gerald's newly assigned role now became evident. Gerald had been the ringleader in the crimes, the assistant DA responded: the number of Gerald's crimes was greater. He would pose a danger if freed, whereas Cheryl had proven her reliability since her release by committing no new offenses.

People who had seen former prosecutor Kivlan at work in a courtroom recognized the look he now directed at the assistant DA. Gerald had also proven himself when he remained free on bail during the two years he spent awaiting trial, Kivlan informed the DA. And weren't the crimes charged to Violet and Cheryl the same as those Gerald was accused of committing? Relentless, Kivlan pressed Rooney with rapid-fire questions, to which the answers came falteringly. There was something undeniably sharp and implacable in the tone of these questions. The elephant in the living room was making its presence known.

If it had been right to make the agreement freeing Cheryl, so that the children's families could have some closure, as the assistant DA had just argued, Kivlan wanted to know, why shouldn't they be interested in closure in Gerald's case?

DA Rooney responded to all these queries with further details of the anguish Gerald had inflicted and the needs of the families and the children. This emphasis apparently moved board member Maureen Walsh, a former prosecutor herself, to put a question of her own: Did Assistant DA Rooney think that perhaps, in addition to the families' needs, society's concern for justice might also be important?

All told, the assistant DA did not have an easy time, and her difficulties were to increase. It was clear, for example, that the argument that Gerald was the ringleader who had committed the most heinous offenses and carried the women along was nowhere borne out in the record of the original trial. To the contrary. In that record, DA Harshbarger had used identical language to describe the crimes alleged against all three members of the Amirault family. Moreover—and it was a point Harshbarger emphasized—he wanted it understood that there were no mitigating circumstances to explain the acts of any of these perpetrators.

As the hearing drew to a close, the board heard from the

Fells Acres parents, there to testify to the pain and suffering that had shadowed their lives as a result of Gerald's crimes. All who spoke testified that no punishment could atone for these crimes, whose effects they lived with every day. In a voice tight with anger, one woman rose to say that Gerald should never be free—that a life sentence would have been appropriate for him. No therapy would ever be enough, said another, to undo the harm done by the Amiraults.

Finally, there came the former Fells Acres pupil, flanked by her parents. This was Jennifer Bennett, who in her first interviews with interrogator Susan Kelley had repeatedly said she had not been touched and continued to say it despite efforts to persuade her that her little friend AJ had already told about bad things that happened. A massively overweight woman of twenty now, she tearfully described the numerous emotional and physical problems afflicting her since she had been victimized. These, she explained, also included her weight problem. Unable to control her tears, her legs shaking convulsively, she begged the board to reject Gerald Amirault's commutation petition. Her embittered father offered a similar statement.

There could be no doubting the parents' conviction that their children had been violated and tortured in a magic room at Fells Acres, or the former child witness's certainty that she had endured unspeakable sexual assaults at her preschool—a belief that was now the defining act of her life and her identity. Her statement done, the young woman's parents sat grimly by as a group of Fells Acres parents surrounded their daughter to offer congratulations.

The proceedings over, the Amirault family filed out, spent, to await the decision that represented the last real hope for Gerald's freedom. It was a slim one, as they knew. There was little in the statistics to encourage hope. Between 1988 and 1997 the board had considered 270 petitions for commutation, of which just 7 had been granted.

The board's decision was a longer time coming than the Amiraults and the attorneys expected. The six-member panel had embarked on what was by any measure one of the most thorough investigations of a commutation or parole applicant in the board's history. There were reasons for this assiduous search apart from the notoriety of the Fells Acres case. The Board of Pardons and Paroles had only a few years earlier recommended parole for Joe Yandle, convicted of first-degree murder for his participation in an armed robbery in 1972. In the mid-1990s, Yandle's case became something of a cause célèbre, thanks to his exceptional reputation as a model prisoner and a veteran who had served his country—one, it was said, who had only been peripherally involved in the crime. In 1995, the board recommended parole for Yandle, only to discover that the prisoner had lied about his service in Vietnam. Back went the parolee to prison. This humiliation caused no small trouble to the parole office's top administration and also guaranteed that those sitting on the board would in the future leave no record uninspected, no route of inquiry unpursued.

The board ran down every prison rumor, every conceivable question that could be raised about Gerald Amirault's comportment in the sixteen years he had been behind bars, exhaustively queried every prison supervisor who had dealt with him. They conducted this investigation for nearly ten months.

When six of those months passed without a word from the board, the Amiraults and Sultan grew increasingly anxious. In that time, George W. Bush had been elected president. There was much speculation in Massachusetts about what this might mean for Governor Cellucci, known to be hankering for a job in the new administration. The governor was, in due course, appointed ambassador to Canada.

In June 2001, some nine months after the hearing, the Governor's Board of Pardons delivered a unanimous ruling calling for the commutation of Gerald's sentence. Citing issues of fundamental fairness, the board members based their decision on the severity of the sentence meted out to Gerald as compared with those of Violet and Cheryl. By itself, this would have sufficed to make front-page news in Boston, as it did. What made the board's ruling more newsworthy yet was an additional statement by a majority of the board concerning the justice of the convictions and the issue of guilt or innocence—precisely those matters board members were not supposed to consider in their deliberations.

They had complied with those guidelines, the majority noted. "It must be acknowledged, however, that it is clearly a matter of public knowledge that, at the minimum, real and substantial doubt exists concerning petitioner's conviction." The majority went on to note the lack of physical evidence. They referred as well to the charges against the Amiraults, which they described as "extraordinary, if not bizarre allegations." Convictions in similar cases around the country had been discredited thanks to investigations like the one in this case, the statement continued. "It is undeniable that it was in the context of this mounting doubt that the court revoked and revised" codefendant LeFave's sentence without opposition from the Office of the District Attorney. It is also undeniable that it is in the context of this mounting doubt that petitioners' commutation must be considered.

This ruling, which did not simply call for commutation but cast doubt on the entire case, came from a parole board widely acknowledged to be among the toughest in the country.

The prosecutors immediately declared their dismay and

announced that they would oppose Gerald's release. Fells Acres parents expressed their outrage in press interviews. The mother of one child witness told the Boston Globe that Amirault had not been rehabilitated. "He never admitted he did it. As far as I'm concerned he's still sexually dangerous to children. He never got any help in prison." Her son, she said, still suffered from flashbacks. Things were going to be very bad around her house now, another mother predicted.

When she heard news of the board's vote, Patti raced home, overjoyed, to find the family gathered and rejoicing, the press at the door, the phone ringing. She was accustomed to all but the rejoicing, but here it was.

Editorials applauding the board's decision appeared the next day in every major and most minor papers in the state of Massachusetts. The Amiraults had not envisioned anything like this outpouring, but it was in a way not surprising. The sentiments confirmed what they felt in their bones: that everybody now knew what this case was and had for some time. That the only group who still believed that children had been assaulted and terrorized at Fells Acres was a hard core of people who would go to their graves believing in the magic room and all the rest. Among the believers, of course, were the former witnesses, their parents, and perhaps the prosecutors.

There were still hurdles ahead before Gerald could be set

free. The board's decision had to be approved by Cellucci's former lieutenant governor, now the acting governor, Jane Swift. In the normal course of events, it was to be expected that the governor would approve the ruling of the Board of Pardons—a ruling that had come after months of investigation into every aspect of Gerald Amirault's history. The worry now for Sultan and the Amiraults was not that Acting Governor Swift was an unknown factor; even at this early stage of her stewardship, she had already developed a solid reputation for vacillation and a certain cluelessness. A decided confusion about the perquisites of office—evident in her use of statehouse employees to do her baby-sitting—got her into trouble, as did her personal use of the state helicopter. The list of her difficulties was long.

Still, Swift was not so clueless as to overlook the public sympathy uniquely available to her as America's only pregnant governor. She soon became the mother of twins, an event that propelled countless pictures of the radiant mother and her infants onto the TV screens and the papers.

The acting governor's poll numbers nevertheless continued to drop. Among the issues confronting her in the midst of all this was the Board of Pardon's ruling on Gerald Amirault. Sought out for comment the day of the ruling, Swift announced that she would look carefully at the recommendation. A day later, her representatives announced that the governor would make the decision "in her own time." There was something faintly disquieting in the tone of this declaration, but Gerald and his family felt they understood. The acting governor had to establish a sense of her authority.

Meanwhile, the District Attorney's office was not idle. To persuade the governor to override the Board of Pardon's ruling, DA Martha Coakley set up meetings between the governor and the former child witnesses, their parents, and like-minded advocates. The DA also summoned local reporters to a special interview. The commonwealth prosecutors had evidently come to the conclusion, justifiably enough, that their side of the Amirault case was not coming off well in the press coverage. This state of affairs, Coakley told reporters, was probably the result of the fact that the Amiraults' victims had remained too much in the background. The DA accordingly presented three former pupils who told of the terrifying attacks they suffered at the hands of Violet, Cheryl, and Gerald Amirault. They were there now, they made clear, to voice their outrage at the possibility of Gerald's release.

The three accusers meeting the press were roughly four years old when they were first interrrogated by investigators. One of the three was twenty-one-year-old Brian Martinello, whose mother was also present to give reporters a list of abuse symptoms she said she had noticed in her son seventeen years earlier. Brian declared Gerald Amirault guilty of disgusting crimes, telling reporters that it was an absolute disgrace to let such a person out of prison.

The investigators encountered nothing like such certainty in 1984 when they questioned Brian, then four years old. The child was interrogated eight times in three weeks, and, as the interview record shows, none of it was easy going for investigators looking for disclosures of abuse.

"A bad guy called Steve" had taken them to Boston in a big black car, the child informed them. Also, "Miss Vi" (Violet Amirault) had made him eat a frog, the frog tasted like salad, and it went quack-quack. Violet Amirault wore a wicked witch dress, the boy reported. Miss Vi had also scratched him with her fingernails and stuck a knife inside him. At the end of the session, Brian asked someone to pin on his junior police badge, a gift often given to encourage children to talk and give them the feeling they were helping police.

Also appearing at the press conference was Phaedra Hopkins, another former witness. The record of her early interviews showed she repeatedly denied that anyone had molested her at Fells Acres. An interviewer noted that the child was subjected to much prodding by her mother because of these continued denials.

Former Fells Acres witness Jennifer Bennett wept bitterly

here, as at the commutation hearing. As a child, she told reporters, she had wakened screaming, thinking her bed was on fire, which Violet and Cheryl and Gerald all threatened would happen if she reported them. "This family raped me, molested me, and totally ruined my life."

It was impossible to miss the continual references to the terrifying Miss Vi and Cheryl as rapists and molesters, assailants often mentioned more frequently than Gerald in these denunciations. The former Fells Acres students brought together this day specifically to oppose commutation for Gerald had apparently not caught up with the official new narrative of events that made Gerald the primary offender.

The governor's inquiry into the commutation question was to be conducted by her former legal adviser, Leonard Lewin, who quickly busied himself visiting Gerald, conferring with prison officials on Gerald's character and history. The Amiraults, Gerald included, took encouragement from Lewin's energetic inquiries and interested questions. Gerald's daughters, Katie and Gerrilyn, reacted with exhilaration when Lewin asked them confidentially how they would feel about their father being released and able to live at home with them, but with certain conditions attached—perhaps having to wear an electronic bracelet.

Patti took encouragement from a meeting with Swift,

who asked the children questions. The governor seemed warm and direct, and had looked her and the children in the eye when talking to them. There was a good feeling in that office, Patti reported to the family. It felt right.

The governor held meetings as well with the Fells Acres witnesses and their families and others lobbying to keep Gerald in prison. Months having passed with no action on the commutation, Sultan now began placing regular calls asking Lewin when a decision could be expected. Lewin assured him all was proceeding normally. No announcement was imminent, but he wanted to issue one warning: that he, Lewin, detested the press, and so did the governor, certainly where this matter was concerned, and that Sultan would be well advised to discourage stories about this issue if he had his client's interest at heart.

On February 20, 2002, six months after the Board of Pardon's unanimous vote, Swift delivered her decision. After a comprehensive review, she and her staff had decided that commutation for Gerald Amirault was, in the words of the official statement, "not warranted." The governor offered little more detail than that as reporters pressed for her reasons. She could not tell them how she came to her conclusion, she told the press, because she had promised anonymity to the people who came to her to argue against commutation.

The governor had few more comments other than to say

that she and her aides had conducted a much more thorough examination than had the Board of Pardons and Paroles. The governor in addition told reporters that she had reviewed almost 100 child rape cases and had been helped to her conclusions by looking at the case of the infamous Christopher Reardon, a twenty-four-year-old youth worker and self-confessed child molester charged with the rape of twenty-nine boys. The comparison between Gerald and Reardon outraged no one more than Isaac Borenstein, the sentencing judge who had given Reardon forty to fifty years. In this case, prosecutors had no trouble getting a guilty plea, given their evidence, which included videotapes of Reardon engaging in sexual acts with one of the boys and computer listings on which he had recorded physical details of the children he molested.

More than a few journalists were prepared for the likelihood that the governor might deny Gerald's commutation. With her poll numbers sinking and rumors spreading that state Republicans wanted the newly popular Mitt Romney, manager for cleansing and general moral improvement at the Salt Lake City Winter Olympics, to replace her in the fall gubernatorial race, it was expected that Swift would weigh any move that might cost her politically. One of the governor's aides put the issue clearly, telling a Boston Herald reporter on background that the governor knew there would be a backlash if she denied the commutation, but she feared the backlash would be stronger from the other side.

Even so, few were prepared for comments as transparent as those she now offered for denying Gerald Amirault's commutation. It was clear from the crudity and heedlessness of her arguments—the effort to link Gerald with Reardon being just one—that the governor and her aides well knew that her decision would be seen for what it was: a cold political calculation. Gerald Amirault's was a spotless record. The toughest parole board in the country had not only recommended that his sentence be commuted, a majority of the members had obviously concluded that he was the victim of a wrongful prosecution. Most of the legal establishment now saw the Amirault case as a travesty of justice. The evidence for this view was overwhelming.

What could the governor do confronted with such facts? Clearly Jane Swift and her aides understood the uselessness of efforts to summon credible arguments for the decision she wanted to make. They decided, therefore, to make none. The response would be what it would be, and it would be done.

In this spirit, the governor went forth to state that she had conducted a more thorough investigation than the Board of Pardons had. That she had considered the terrible nature of the charges and estimated the harmful effect commutation would have on the victims. Her investigation of Gerald Amirault's record of behavior while in prison had led her to the conclusion that he had made no "exceptional strides in self-development." Queried repeatedly about this claim—Gerald's exemplary behavior record was no secret—the governor declined to answer. She didn't want to go through the whole thing and begin reviewing, she informed reporters.

The governor profited little by her decision to keep Gerald in prison. A Massachusetts poll taken immediately after her announcement showed a majority opposed to Swift's decision to override the Board of Pardons.

A bit over a month later, a tearful Governor Swift announced she would not be the gubernatorial candidate and would be leaving office. The governor then issued a statement that was, in spirit, not unlike the one denying Gerald Amirault's commutation. In the face of all facts to the contrary, the acting governor offered as her reasons the claims of motherhood. She was sure every working parent had faced her problem, Swift declared. "When the demands of two tasks that you take on both increase substantially, something has to give." What had actually increased substantially was, of course, Mitt Romney's standing in the approval polls: Acting Governor Swift was now running something like 60 percent behind him. Everyone knew the reason she left the field, and the governor knew that they knew.

In her brief tenure, she had nonetheless left her mark, and it was an ineradicable one. With one politically driven decision, she had closed the door to freedom as Gerald Amirault was about to walk through it.

It was not the absolute last chance. James Sultan, Ogletree, and Silverglate determined that Gerald could petition the Board of Pardons for early parole—the same board that granted him commutation. Unlike commutation, the grant of parole required no permission from the governor.

Before the grant of another hearing before the board, there were certain hurdles to pass—those established by the Massachusetts Department of Corrrections, which had panels of its own to determine whether an inmate merited parole.

The panel assigned to Gerald's case made a speedy determination. The three-man board decided that since the prisoner had refused participation in treatment programs for sex offenders, they considered him "in denial." He was therefore to be denied permission to appear before the Board of Pardons to request early parole.

The thinking guiding the panel was clear enough. The prisoner had been convicted by a jury; he was therefore guilty. The only justification for parole was proof that the criminal had been rehabilitated. Rehabilitation required acknowledgment of criminality. The worldview governing the

Department of Corrections did not allow for possibilities like wrongful convictions. Thus, Gerald's unvarying assertions of innocence, made at whatever cost to his hopes for parole, was now translated into "failure to take responsibility," as the panel put it.

For the Amiraults, ever capable of optimism even when they had little reason to feel any—which is to say, through nearly all the years of their struggles—this was the moment that finally proved too much. The Amirault who never shed a tear, the sports-obsessed, undemonstrative P.J., was the first to break. For days following the panel decision, he sat wracked by sobs. For Patti Amirault, it was a new thing to see her son thus, and a bitter one.

In eighteen months, Gerald would be eligible for regular parole. He could do eighteen months more. In eighteen months, the panel would again ask about the treatment programs for sex offenders he still would not have entered, the admission of guilt—proof he had "taken responsibility"—he would not have given, and never would.

Two slender chances remained that Gerald might be allowed to go before the Board of Pardon. The chief administrator of Gerald's prison, the Bay State Correctional Facility, had the power to overrule the three-man panel and permit the petition, as could the state commissioner of corrections. Gerald requested a meeting with the Bay State administrator, who told him in May that he would consider the matter. The administrator was cordial. He would get back to him, he told Gerald, when he returned from vacation.

———

In September 1997, eleven years after Grant Snowden's conviction and imprisonment, the Eleventh U.S. Circuit Court of Appeals heard oral arguments in the case of Grant Snowden. Robert Rosenthal, his new appellate attorney, presented the case for reversal of conviction. The prosecutors' response to this event was telling testimony to the security the state had enjoyed with regard to this case. This was clear in the opening address by Assistant Attorney General Roberta Mandel, who began by telling the three-judge panel of her astonishment that a federal court could now be hearing further arguments about this case. Indeed, the prosecutor informed Judges Harry Wellford, J. L. Edmondson, and Thomas A. Clark, she didn't know what she was even doing up there—a comment that brought a sharp retort from at least one judge.

The remarks of the assistant attorney general should have surprised no one acquainted with the history of the Snowden case—a history that could only have nurtured the prosecutors' faith that nothing would ever undo this conviction. In a decade of state appeals, nothing—not the quantities of hearsay allowed into evidence nor the records showing the state's agent putting accusations in the children's mouths, not the false claims of medical evidence nor the trial's numerous similar features that virtually ensured a verdict of guilty—had ever moved any Florida court to take a second look at this conviction. It was perfectly reasonable for the assistant attorney general to behave as if there were something approaching the unnatural about this court proceeding. Never before had the prosecutors been required to address serious questions about this case.

One of the three federal appeals court judges now asked how it could have happened that the prosecutors could have put before the jury expert witnesses who vouched that the testimony of the accusing children was true. It was a question the assistant attorney general had some difficulty answering. To use authorities like expert witnesses to tell a jury that other witnesses are telling the truth—to say to jurors, thus, that the accused is guilty (or innocent)—is strictly prohibited, a bedrock violation of due process. The actual answer, which the assistant attorney general could not offer, was clear enough: they did it because the trial judge allowed it.

While the oral argument took place, former officer Snowden, Prisoner No. 102495, busied himself at his job, running the prison canteen at South Bay Correctional Facility, work that kept him busy all day, tired him, kept his mind focused on the external world. The job had been hard won but well worth it. Snowden now depended on the canteen for his peace of mind and valued his work there above any privilege available to him.

When the story of his prosecution and trial first appeared in The Wall Street Journal in 1997, Grant Snowden had been behind bars eleven years. As the Amiraults and Kelly Michaels and others incarcerated in these cases discovered, the press spotlight almost invariably improved their standing in prison, and not only among the inmates. Prison personnel tended to treat the prisoner in question with a certain caution at least, if not with sympathy.

That would not happen in Snowden's case. With the publication of that 1997 piece, his supervisors at Avon Park revoked all the privileges he had won as a long-time prisoner, including a cell of his own. His offense, one of them told him, was his failure to warn prison officials about a story to come. For this, he was placed in solitary for a day; when he came out, he was informed he no longer had his job running the canteen. He would now have to start all over. With little faith in court action and challenges of his conviction, he gave virtually no thought to the possibilities of freedom. His future was the prison. All that had made life there tolerable—the privileges accorded a senior prisoner, the job that had made his days bearable, busy, and focused on the present—were gone.

A year later, all of it would be irrelevant. On March 26, 1998, promptly at 11 A.M., former police officer Grant Snowden strode through the doors of the sprawling U.S. District Court for the Southern District of Florida, surrounded by federal marshals and state guards. As he came into view, the crowd of family members and friends pacing outside Courtroom 10 surged forward, his youngest brother clenching hands to his temple, his sister calling his name. The prisoner looked straight ahead. A jot of the police officer still in him, he joined his voice to those of the marshals telling everyone to stand back.

Eyes fixed on the procession sweeping past, the family members stood clumped together, breathless simply at the sight of their brother, their son, and their father, out in the world again. For how long, they had no idea.

He was here this morning because the Eleventh U.S. Circuit Court of Appeals had overturned his conviction a few weeks earlier. Appellate attorney Robert Rosenthal had won a habeas corpus victory all the more remarkable for the rarity, nowadays, of such victories.

The prosecutors announced at once that the state would fight the reversal all the way. Further, Assistant Attorney General Michael Neimand announced, his office would strenuously oppose any effort to release the prisoner on bail. Whether the state's attorneys would succeed in the effort to keep Grant Snowden in prison while they appealed the appeals court's decision or whether the judge would defer a decision on bail (in essence leaving Snowden at liberty pending a new trial), as many prognosticators guessed he would, was the question before the court this day.

The answer was not long in coming. Shortly after the crowd filed into the courtroom, there were indications things might not go as the state wished. Flanked by Rosenthal, who made the argument for bail, and his Florida lawyer, Arthur Cohen, Grant Snowden sat and listened, along with everyone else, as the assistant attorney general instructed the judge in the reasons this court had no authority to grant bail. Judge William C. Turnoff listened affably as Assistant Attorney General Neimand offered his argument. When that was over, the judge turned to Snowden.

He had never been convicted of any crime before these charges had come along, had he? asked the judge, clearly versed in the details of the case.

He had not.

And how long had he spent in prison? the judge asked.

"Twelve years, your honor."

The question struck a nerve, as did the answer. Up near

into the girl's vagina, the nurse testified, this was proof that the girl had been penetrated—a dubious conclusion, given all the other physical possibilities, as the defense gynecologist would point out. It was one, in any event, there was no way to verify, the nurse having decided not to photograph her examination. Instead, she sent the report off to Detective Weber, who informed the girl that she was no longer a virgin.

Next, the girl was sent to state trooper Edward Girtler, who was, as he would later acknowledge, immediately certain that Carroll was guilty. Confiding only in Detective Weber, he decided to have the girl make a taped phone call in which she confronted Carroll—an enterprise that did not work out as they had planned.

In the course of the monitored call, the detective prompted the girl, giving her questions and reminder notes about what she was to say, all of which, the detective hoped, would lead to incriminating statements of recognition, pleas for secrecy.

The girl began by telling Carroll she was frightened.

CARROLL: What are you scared of, honey?

GIRL: Because Mommy's taking me to the gynecologist.

CARROLL: Yeah, so what are you afraid of? Huh? Nobody's around, you can talk to me.

the magistrate's bench, tears gleamed in the eyes of a court attendant—not the only one in the room in this condition.

The judge announced he would grant bail ($50,000, secured by family property) and set some standard restrictions governing travel and curfew.

The judge asked what additonal restrictions the state might want to impose on Snowden. The state did have one urgent request: that Snowden be prohibited from talking to the press and television people when released. Hearing it, spectators turned to gape at one another. Unlike District Attorney Martha Coakley in Massachusetts, Florida's prosecutors didn't worry exclusively about television interviews; they wanted Snowden barred from talking to anyone in the press.

Judge Turnoff dryly informed the assistant attorney general that he didn't think this encroachment on First Amendment rights would be quite in order.

An hour after the court session ended, the released prisoner and his lawyers came walking through the door. All that remained now was a trip to the holding center for final paperwork. Snowden stepped into the bright glare of a Miami day, lean, with a still-quick smile, and auburn hair as his prison ID described it: an attractive man at fifty-one even in the shambling suit someone had thought to bring on the chance things turned out as they did.

John Carroll

By the late 1990s, with the exception of the Amiraults of Massachusetts, whose Supreme Judicial Court continued to find no serious miscarriage of justice, the convictions in all such headline-making cases of mass abuse had been thrown out by appeals courts around the nation. There would be no more such trials, no more TV journalists standing in front of closed nursery schools delivering solemn reports on the horrors that had taken place therein—children dragged to graveyards to be abused, to secret rooms, four and five year olds forced to eat boiled babies, or feces. Still, the fantastic trials had left their legacy. Every schoolchild now knew, as did every embittered spouse, the matchless power of a child molestation charge.

In 1997, John Carroll, a marina owner who lived in Troy, New York, was charged with the abuse and rape of his thirteen-year-old stepdaughter and convicted at trial. Eileen Treacy would serve as an expert witness for the prosecution at his second trial. The passage of time had in some respects broadened her horizons. Instead of the thirty-two behavioral indicators of abuse she had defined at Kelly Michaels's 1987 trial, she now had sixty-six.

The charges against Carroll began with a dream the girl had that someone had been touching her—the person being, she reported, a young male cousin. Others suggested to her that the events in the dream had actually taken place, but the girl insisted it was a dream. After much questioning by Carroll's estranged wife and by the wife's friend, the girl was persuaded the dream was reality. John Carroll, her stepfather, was the person charged with touching her sexually.

The mother took her daughter to see Troy detective Steven Weber, who would take on a peculiar dual role as investigator and expert witness. The detective took the girl's statement and arranged for her to have a physical exam. The examiner to whom he sent the alleged victim was, as it happened, also the detective's girlfriend. Jane Szary, a nurse practitioner, would provide a report that made claims far more serious than the "touching" reported to the detective. Because she had room to insert a speculum and two fingers the magistrate's bench, tears gleamed in the eyes of a court attendant—not the only one in the room in this condition.

The judge announced he would grant bail ($50,000, secured by family property) and set some standard restrictions governing travel and curfew.

The judge asked what additonal restrictions the state might want to impose on Snowden. The state did have one urgent request: that Snowden be prohibited from talking to the press and television people when released. Hearing it, spectators turned to gape at one another. Unlike District Attorney Martha Coakley in Massachusetts, Florida's prosecutors didn't worry exclusively about television interviews; they wanted Snowden barred from talking to anyone in the press.

Judge Turnoff dryly informed the assistant attorney general that he didn't think this encroachment on First Amendment rights would be quite in order.

An hour after the court session ended, the released prisoner and his lawyers came walking through the door. All that remained now was a trip to the holding center for final paperwork. Snowden stepped into the bright glare of a Miami day, lean, with a still-quick smile, and auburn hair as his prison ID described it: an attractive man at fifty-one even in the shambling suit someone had thought to bring on the chance things turned out as they did.

John Carroll

By the late 1990s, with the exception of the Amiraults of Massachusetts, whose Supreme Judicial Court continued to find no serious miscarriage of justice, the convictions in all such headline-making cases of mass abuse had been thrown out by appeals courts around the nation. There would be no more such trials, no more TV journalists standing in front of closed nursery schools delivering solemn reports on the horrors that had taken place therein—children dragged to graveyards to be abused, to secret rooms, four and five year olds forced to eat boiled babies, or feces. Still, the fantastic trials had left their legacy. Every schoolchild now knew, as did every embittered spouse, the matchless power of a child molestation charge.

In 1997, John Carroll, a marina owner who lived in Troy, New York, was charged with the abuse and rape of his thirteen-year-old stepdaughter and convicted at trial. Eileen Treacy would serve as an expert witness for the prosecution at his second trial. The passage of time had in some respects broadened her horizons. Instead of the thirty-two behavioral indicators of abuse she had defined at Kelly Michaels's 1987 trial, she now had sixty-six.

The charges against Carroll began with a dream the girl had that someone had been touching her—the person being, she reported, a young male cousin. Others suggested to her that the events in the dream had actually taken place, but the girl insisted it was a dream. After much questioning by Carroll's estranged wife and by the wife's friend, the girl was persuaded the dream was reality. John Carroll, her stepfather, was the person charged with touching her sexually.

The mother took her daughter to see Troy detective Steven Weber, who would take on a peculiar dual role as investigator and expert witness. The detective took the girl's statement and arranged for her to have a physical exam. The examiner to whom he sent the alleged victim was, as it happened, also the detective's girlfriend. Jane Szary, a nurse practitioner, would provide a report that made claims far more serious than the "touching" reported to the detective. Because she had room to insert a speculum and two fingers into the girl's vagina, the nurse testified, this was proof that the girl had been penetrated—a dubious conclusion, given all the other physical possibilities, as the defense gynecologist would point out. It was one, in any event, there was no way to verify, the nurse having decided not to photograph her examination. Instead, she sent the report off to Detective Weber, who informed the girl that she was no longer a virgin.

Next, the girl was sent to state trooper Edward Girtler, who was, as he would later acknowledge, immediately certain that Carroll was guilty. Confiding only in Detective Weber, he decided to have the girl make a taped phone call in which she confronted Carroll—an enterprise that did not work out as they had planned.

In the course of the monitored call, the detective prompted the girl, giving her questions and reminder notes about what she was to say, all of which, the detective hoped, would lead to incriminating statements of recognition, pleas for secrecy.

The girl began by telling Carroll she was frightened.

CARROLL: What are you scared of, honey?

GIRL: Because Mommy's taking me to the gynecologist.

CARROLL: Yeah, so what are you afraid of? Huh? Nobody's around, you can talk to me.

GIRL: Because of the things you've done to me.

CARROLL: Me? Me? What the hell did I do to you? I never did anything to you! What are you talking about, honey?

GIRL: Well, lately I've been remembering things from when I was little.

CARROLL: Oh, my god, honey, I never did anything to you! Me? Jesus! Jesus, I never touched you.

GIRL: Yeah you did.

CARROLL: No sweetheart, I never did. What are you talking about?

GIRL: You did a couple of weeks ago!

CARROLL: I did nothing to you! I rubbed your back, I rubbed your stomach, I rubbed your shoulders. I never touched you in a bad way.

GIRL: Yeah you have.

CARROLL: No! My God! I love you like my daughter, I would never do that to you.

The phone call continues along the same lines, all of it clear evidence of a man in profound shock at the accusations. The detectives immediately understood that the taped call would undercut their case. For the same reason, the prosecutors vehemently opposed its admission into evidence at Carroll's first trial. In this effort, they were successful and free to claim, as they did, that the defendant never denied the crime. The jury could not know about the tape. The prosecutor was free to emphasize in her summation to the jury that the defendant never once said he never touched the child.

Robert Rosenthal signed on as Carroll's defense attorney and succeeded in winning a reversal. The New York Court of Appeals overturned Carroll's conviction in November 2000, but this was far from the end of his problems. The Rensselaer County prosecutors had no intention of dropping this case, which they now planned to retry, notwithstanding certain complications. The tape of the phone call would have to be allowed into evidence, the appeals court having made clear that irreparable error had been done by its exclusion in the first trial.

There were other problems too, among them improbable accusations, including the one that had Carroll molesting the girl in front of a large ground-floor picture window facing a busy street.

As so often, the prosecutors turned to authorities who could explain and render the improbable reasonable. They turned to Eileen Treacy. The most important prosecution witness at the trial of Kelly Michaels, Treacy and her testimony were also chief among the reasons for the reversal of conviction in that case. As prosecutors of the Amiraults did when they introduced a postal inspector to testify to the horrors of child pornography—so that jurors could infer that the Amiraults were guilty of this crime, though there was no such charge against them and no such evidence—Treacy had described behaviors indicative of child sex abuse. She had done so in ways that clearly served to show jurors they should infer that Kelly Michaels's Wee Care students showed exactly the same symptoms and should be seen as victims of abuse.

It is the function of qualified experts to educate jurors in subjects relevant to a case, whether medical, psychological, or other, that are not normally well known to laypeople. Expert witnesses are emphatically not supposed to bolster the claims of one side or another. The impact of Treacy's prejudicial testimony in the Michaels case was, wrote the justices, "overwhelming." Referring to Treacy's capacity to divine signs of child sex abuse and extract accusations in another case, a New Jersey judge wrote, "I am convinced that Ms. Treacy would have been able to elicit the disclosure [of sexual abuse] from many children his age who had not been abused."

None of this deterred prosecutors from seeking Treacy

out as an expert witness in child sex abuse cases. When they called one another seeking advice on the best expert witness, they were likely to hear that Eileen Treacy was a good bet— she won convictions in these cases.

In the Carroll case, Treacy recited from her store of behavioral symptoms, all of which fit the picture of the plaintiff as an abuse victim and her stepfather as the perpetrator. John Carroll had been as devoted to his stepdaughter as to his own children and continued to treat her as a daughter even after his separation from her mother. The court heard testimony about the warm and supportive relationship Carroll had with his stepdaughter from the time he entered the girl's life when she was two and a half. Treacy explained, as she had at the Michaels trial, that kindness, affection, and expressions of friendship were all part of the abuser's typical behavior.

Detective Weber and Trooper Girtler were on hand as well to provide services as expert witnesses, their expertise residing mainly in such matters as body language and subtler signals still, from which they could read indicators of Carroll's guilt.

All of this followed from the problem of the monitored phone call. With the tape now allowed into evidence, the police and prosecutor could no longer claim that Carroll had never denied his guilt. His anguished denials rang loud and clear as the tape was played for the jury.

Girtler and Weber proved equal to the task before them. In this phone call, Girtler informed the jury, there were signs—red flags—of guilt that an untrained person would never notice. True, he conceded, Carroll had denied the accusations, but he had done so in ways that only proved his guilt. For example, he had responded to the stepdaughter's accusation by saying he had never touched her in a bad or sexual way. This, Girtler said, indicated the mind-set of a child molester.

Weber explained that Carroll used words and phrases in that call such as "no," "gee whiz," "oh God!" By his reference to a higher power, Weber explained, he was admitting guilt.

In all, the two experts informed jurors, the phone call showed Carroll making "admission by denial." It was Girtler's view that all of Carroll's denials were evidence of his guilt.

Carroll's body language was, in Weber's view, a serious indicator of guilt. Expertise in this field was not easily come by, he informed jurors. It was not written; "it is something you observe. It is not something you speak. It is something you have to observe with a keen eye."

At one point in the interrogation, Girtler told jurors, Carroll sat himself turning somewhat and "facing the door a little bit"—an indicator he wanted to get out. Carroll's body language indicated he was concerned and blocking admissions.

In her summation to the jury, the prosecutor cited the importance of Girtler's testimony: that of a trained investigator who knew that the defendant's denials of guilt were actually admissions. He knew what he was listening to, the prosecutor assured the jurors. As with the Amirault case, the prosecutors had used an expert witness—and the judge had allowed it—to do what juries are impaneled to do: namely, decide the guilt of the accused.

The expert witnesses and the power of the child abuse charge proved again an unbeatable combination. Within hours of receiving the judge's charge, on January 24, 2001, the jury came back with a guilty verdict. John Carroll is now serving a sentence of ten to twenty years.

Afterward

When he had done with kisses and embraces on the morning of his release, Grant Snowden pushed his way through the crowd to the car that was to take him back to prison for the final paperwork.

During the long drive in which phones rang incessantly with calls from the press, appellate attorney Robert Rosenthal announced that he was going to turn the things off—but first he would call his office in New York. This caught Snowden's attention. He had been staring out of the window, the dazzling smile long gone. Now he wanted to know about the mobile phone so powerful it could reach New York. Thus did he learn about cell phones, an invention that had escaped his notice of his twelve-year journey through Florida's prisons.

The paperwork took time, what with waits for faxes and official signatures, all of it enough to make the attorneys edgy. The reversal of conviction on a habeas plea had been a victory against impossible odds. While nowhere near the same category of improbable successes, the judge's decision to release Snowden at once came as a deep relief. He could well have been ordered imprisoned, as Snowden and the family had been warned beforehand, until the prosecutors appealed the reversal of conviction.

This unaccustomed smooth sailing explained why, even at this late hour, the lawyers worried that some last-minute obstruction would halt the release.

What, after all, would the state prosecutors *not* do to keep Snowden from being loosed into the world, to do what they feared most? What they feared most was not that this man they proclaimed a dangerous predator would now commit some other terrible crime. What they feared was that he would give press interviews.

Finally it was over, the documents signed. His small bundle of possessions in hand, former officer Snowden paused at the prison exit, head swiveling sharply as a guard walked past. "This was the one," he began to say, in a voice tight with rage—"she was the one." His lawyers steered him quickly to the car, terrified that some word or gesture would give the state its chance.

In the car, Snowden said this guard was the one who had withdrawn running privileges and issued demerits because his foot crossed an inch too far over the line when he ran the exercise track—an explanation delivered in embittered tones and lengthy detail. "Why should she do that?" was the question on his mind, the anger gnawing at him at this, his moment of liberation.

At the homecoming party, Grant stopped suddenly at the fence in front of his mother's house when everyone else in the group walked through. He recognized the reflex. Newly released former prisoners did not walk easily through barricades. Neither would much else come easily now. Still, in his mother's small house crowded with well-wishers, and family members, grandchildren and nieces and nephews all swarming around, he felt a free man again and a happy one, and for the moment, it was enough.

Swarming around, too, were members of the press. The assistant attorney general's worries about all the news this story would make were now about to be borne out, as television reporters crowded the living room, preparing broadcasts on the long-forgotten Snowden case.

In the hours that followed, reporters asked many times over whether he might try again to join the police force, a question that invariably brought vague answers. In private, Snowden made his feelings clearer. He had seen too much at the hands of guards, too much of the system, to want to wear a police uniform again. The former officer who once eagerly worked the night shift because nights were the time of highest criminal activity and arrest numbers now said it was all very simple: he could not bring himself to send other people to prison.

For those falsely charged and imprisoned for long terms, the effects of freedom are unpredictable, harder than anything they imagined in the years behind bars and different in a thousand ways. None of this can they know, of course, at the beginning—the day of release, with rejoicing family and friends and the clamor of reporters inevitably on hand for these occasions. It takes time, after the joy and celebrations and the gratitude for exoneration, to grasp the realities. To be sure, it took virtually no time for the nearly seventy-year-old Violet Amirault to see what her life was to be when she was freed, penniless: no more than two days before she began to murmur that in prison, she at least knew where she was, and what was going to happen the next hour. She had her cubbyhole with all her things, all that she owned where she could lay her hands on it. The feeling did not last long, nor did her life in freedom, such as it was.

For Snowden, the realities of the new life sunk in more slowly, prime among them the trouble he would have finding a job. Because of practices peculiar to Florida's record system, every job interview ended with a computer check showing convictions on charges of child sex abuse, notwithstanding the court's reversal. Despondent at the failure to find work, and a good deal more, he tried to conceal his state of mind from family members, his mother in particular, and his brother, Wendell, who tried to find ways to get Grant moving. He insisted Grant begin driving again, but Snowden, who had driven a truck many years before joining the force, now resisted getting behind the wheel.

Mostly, he resisted talking and showing the signs of depression. He was, after all, supposed to be grateful for his deliverance—exonerated, free, and about to begin to live again. He felt a free man all right, but also a tense one most of the time, aware of his growing anger. As he had before, endlessly, he replayed the year 1984 when it all began—every detail of the charges that had blown his life apart. The difference now was that he was a free man and had begun to think like one—to consider all that had happened and to ask why no one would be held responsible.

In February, his life took a happier turn when he married Donna, a spirited high school government teacher who endured his bouts of pent-up rage with patience and a certain wariness. In addition to all else she brought to the marriage, she had a friendly former husband who also happened to be an attorney. When a letter arrived from the Florida Department of Law Enforcement announcing that Grant Snowden was listed as a sexual predator, that he had to register as one and have his picture distributed in his neighborhood, Mrs. Snowden's former husband undertook to straighten the department out and did. Grant soon received a letter acknowledging the error.

The Snowdens moved to Melrose, Florida, where Donna took a job at a community college, and Grant, now fifty-five, took over management of their small horse farm. He had much to be thankful for, he said after his marriage—his wife, friendship, his family—and would doubtless repeat it today. What he lacks is a way to blot out the past gnawing away at him.

———

The realities of their newfound freedom came early to Carol and Mark Doggett, among the numerous citizens of Wenatchee, Washington, falsely accused of child sex abuse in the mid-1990s. Attorney Robert Rosenthal also undertook the Doggetts' appeal, won in 1997. Afterward, he told the couple, who had served three years of a ten-year, ten-month sentence, that they had about ninety days to enjoy their period of gratitude and exhilaration. After that, the rough times would likely begin.

A little more than a month after their liberation, Mrs. Doggett called the attorney to say she and her husband were ahead of schedule. The hard times had already arrived with their efforts to get the state to return their children, sent to foster care when Mark and Carol were accused of assaulting them sexually. The Doggetts were the ones who supposedly forced their five children to line up outside a bedroom door nightly to await their turn to be raped by their parents.

That was in 1995. Though neither she nor her husband have known many occasions for great joy since their release, there have been a few, not least when the Doggetts saw every one of their children finally returned to them.

The last child allowed home was the youngest, nine years old at the time her parents were tried and now in her teens. Before she could return, a court-appointed psychologist had to examine the girl and her parents, look into the family history, and assess general conditions at home. After concluding her inquiry, the psychologist delivered her report, in which she stated that Carol and Mark Doggett had never molested their children but that the youngest girl had indeed been injured. She had been traumatized, the report concluded, by the forced separation from her parents.

The couple had emerged from prison without funds or credit. Carol, who had graduated from college with a degree in business, found work in a grocery store and then, with the help of a friend, found a position in the computer field. They were luckier than most others, she concluded. They survived, and they reclaimed their children. Mark went on to a job driving a forklift, a job that gives him too much time to think about things. A tall man with an easy manner, he is preoccupied with one thing: that there should be justice, an idea seldom far from his mind. Or Grant Snowden's.

The prosecutors, the investigators, the expert witnesses, the accusers, remained untouched. For them, there were no consequences, Doggett observes, no consequences after all the trumped-up prosecutions, people thrown into prison, children ruined.

It was a common enough response. Like most other accused citizens, he had had faith in the legal system and in the protections guaranteed by the Constitution. So, too, had Grant Snowden and the Amiraults. They believed that democracy and fairness and the American system would see them through—would ensure that a jury could not possibly believe lies and wild stories of the kind offered as evidence against them. When they were convicted and sentenced, they knew that innocent citizens could be found guilty of horrible crimes they never dreamed of, that they could be separated from society and sent away—in the case of some falsely accused, to multiple life terms.

Even so, an ingrained belief in justice is not easily abandoned. When they emerged from prison, it was justice they sought, even as they understood that they would find none. They understood, and it haunted them, that there would be no consequences to the prosecutors and the investigators— and still they thought of justice.

———

Cheryl Amirault has her mind on other matters, mainly her brother and her job. For her the days have only one focus: work. The mornings are not wonderful, but the nights are worse. Her dreams—her nightmares—are almost always the same: she and her mother and brother are all back together, running the Fells Acres Day School. The atmosphere is playful and they are happy, with children running all about, but there is a feeling of dread too, which grows as the dream continues. The children play, her mother is there, as she always was, confident, in charge, and busy. Yet Cheryl is terrified and keeps running to the windows, afraid that the police are coming for some reason, and they always do.

Nothing for Cheryl Amirault is quite right until she arrives at her job. Work was her curative since the Amiraults were first charged, and so it remains. Today she works with customers at John Hancock Financial Services. She arrived as an office temporary and was soon hired full time, all the while wondering whether her bosses and coworkers knew anything about her and what they would say if they did.

She found out, soon enough, when she had been employed at the company six months. In late 1999, the day after a detailed media story on the case, she was called to the office of two company directors, a summons she answered trembling with apprehension. Their message was brief. They wanted to tell her that they were proud to have her as an employee and that they wanted her to know that.

At her desk she found a flood of similar e-mail from company employees. In addition to all else this meant, it was, she knew, a measure of the credibility people now ascribed to the prosecutors' charges against the Amiraults.

One day in the year 2000, she awoke feeling strangely rested. It came to her that she had just passed the first night in memory without a nightmare.

Gerald Amirault remains a prisoner of the Commonwealth of Massachusetts, whose commissioner of prisons turned down his appeal for an early appearance before the parole board. The commissioner, who, like Acting Governor Jane Swift, saw similarities between the case of Gerald Amirault and that of a confessed mass child molester by the name of Reardon, noted that Gerald Amirault had shown no signs of progress toward his rehabilitation.

EPILOGUE

Over the years, certain queries about these cases came up so often their frequency was hard to ignore. They were telling questions. Leading the pack—the question readers, commentators, and everyone else paying attention to the history of these prosecutions wanted answered—was, What did the prosecutors think? Did they actually believe in the charges they had brought, of naked children tied to trees in full public view and raped in broad daylight, as in the Amirault case; in the testimony of child witnesses who had recited obvious whoppers about robots, being stabbed with swords, and the like?

A reasonable question. One for which there is no answer other than that some did, some did not, and either way it hardly mattered. The prosecutors' propensity to believe in the guilt of anyone accused of the crime of child sex abuse was overwhelming. That belief was fueled by investigators who shared the same propensity and interrogated the children accordingly. The children had themselves come forth with their accusations, and had done so all on their own, so the investigators said: children would not make up such accusations out of nothing.

This thinking, combined with the overweening hunger to win convictions, argues powerfully against the likelihood that prosecutors sat up nights during the Amiraults' trials or those of others like them, worrying about the truth of the charges. If any there were who actually harbored such concerns, they managed, quite successfully, to conceal them.

Shortly after a jury convicted Kelly Michaels in 1988, a Los Angeles Times reporter put a question to the victorious prosecutors, Glenn Goldberg and Sara McArdle. He was curious about certain of the charges, said the journalist—things like the accused inserting knives into childrens' ears and such. Did they, the prosecutors, actually believe that kind of story?

No, Glenn Goldberg answered.

Oh, absolutely, came the reply from prosecutor McArdle.

Both had answered at the same instant—doubtless a moment of revelation for Sara McArdle.

How jurors could have believed child witnesses who had given clearly fantastic testimony—another question often asked—was easier to answer. The state's expert witnesses, the psychologists and the abuse specialists, were on hand precisely to provide the explanation for such testimony. Some, like Eileen Treacy, traveled from trial to trial validating charges of abuse.

Their explanation: the children had been traumatized and tortured and, as a result, had had to construct all sorts of fantasies to defend themselves. Jurors were little inclined to doubt the experts. And there was the fact that the children had given specific descriptions of their abuse. How such claims came to be made the jurors did not know.

In the course of their pretrial interrogations, the children in the Kelly Michaels case were given knives and forks and anatomically correct dolls. They were then asked to show where their teacher had hurt them. Confused, but obedient, the preschooler poked at the doll's head, or neck, or arms, all locations obviously unsatisfactory to the interviewer, who kept asking, "Where else?"

Finally the child would touch the doll's sex organs—the moment for which the interviewer had been waiting, for which the entire exercise had been designed. Here all urgings to say "where else" ended. The interviewer now wrote up notes attesting to the child's disclosure, and saying that the victim had described how he or she had been penetrated. This would be the testimony presented to the jurors.

Defense lawyers could argue, and some did, vociferously,

that the interviewers had spent months leading the children and putting accusations in their mouths. But these arguments could not prevail against the spectacle of four- and five-year-old witnesses who had come forward to say that they had been tortured. They could not prevail against the summations, in which prosecutors begged jurors not to betray the faith of the little ones who had come to tell their stories: they must not deliver a verdict that would declare these children liars.

Once the first charge was made and investigations began, parents of children being questioned found their lives transformed. Those whose children were to become plaintiffs (not all parents were willing to allow their child to become involved) were now bound by a common passion to see the offenders convicted; they sought one another out; they shared with one another details of comments they had extracted from their children. Tortured as the parents were by the thought of the outrages committed against their children, they found, in the society of others they saw as victims like themselves, a powerful bond—and in the case itself, a drama that utterly absorbed them. They lived their lives with a focus and intensity previously unknown to them as they prepared for the trials and consulted with prosecutors and therapists. Of the principals in these cases, none were to believe the charges more immediately or more everlastingly than the parents.

Finally, I have to note the query often raised in the course of interviews about these cases. Did I recognize that child sex abuse existed and was a serious problem? reporters would ask. A strange question, that. The discussion of no other crime would require such a disclaimer. Journalists who have written about false murder charges are seldom asked to provide reassurances that they know murder is a bad thing, and it really happens.

The question attests to the political fear attaching to the subject of child abuse, particularly the proposition that children's accusations are not invariably truthful. Governor Jane Swift would know something about political fear of that kind. So, too, would prisoner of the Commonwealth of Massachusetts Gerald Amirault.

INDEX

Index

ABOUT THE AUTHOR

Dorothy Rabinowitz, winner of the 2001 Pulitzer Prize in commentary, is a member of the editorial board and a culture critic for The Wall Street Journal. She writes opinion pieces and television criticism for the paper. Prior to joining the Journal, Ms. Rabinowitz was an independent writer. Her work has appeared in numerous publications, including Commentary, Harper's Magazine, and New York. She is the author of *New Lives,* a study of survivors of the Nazi death camps, and has been a syndicated columnist and television commentator. She lives in New York City.